Monographic Journals of the Near East *Afroasiatic Linguistics* 8/4 (December 1982)

BIBLIOGRAPHIC BULLETIN

TABLE OF CONTENTS

I. REVIEWS

A. F. L. Beeston, *Samples of Arabic Prose in its Historical Development* (A Manual for English-speaking Students). London: Oxford University Press, 1977, 47 pp., $4.00.
By CHARLES WENDELL† (University of California, Santa Barbara)

This small monograph is the third in a series of works addressed by the author to the student of Arabic. It consists of twenty-eight selections ranging in time from the seventh to the twentieth century, each prefaced by remarks about the author and the significant features of his style, and followed by Professor Beeston's translation of the piece. An introduction furnishes the reader with a capsule history of Arabic prose and its evolution during this time, though for further clarification, he would be well advised to consult Beeston's article "Parallelism in Arabic prose" in the *Journal of Arabic Literature* 5:134-146. One can hardly quarrel with the author over the selections themselves: they are certainly representative of the several genres known to the writers of Arabic up to very recent times, when the influence of the West becomes pervasive and there are unprecedented innovations in both style and genre. He may have been right in omitting any Qur'ānic excerpts. The Book is probably best dealt with in isolation, though I myself am of the Wellhausenian conviction that the best surviving examples of the *kāhin*'s art are the *sūra*s of the Early Meccan period. The few remaining pagan utterances in *saj*ʿ are too short, dry and lacking in interior interest for inclusion in a work of this type. As long as the same term (*saj*ʿ) is used of the two modes, however, one or two of the early *sūra*s with their fine archaic power would have been the perfect contrast for the intensely stylized and rococo extravagances of Badīʿ al-Zamān and Al-Ḥarīrī in their *maqāmāt*. But this apart, I have no complaints about the choice and indeed feel that Professor Beeston has made a very good one.

He is perhaps overoptimistic when he describes the work as one "intended for the undergraduate student of Arabic". I do not think that the greater number of undergraduate students of Arabic–in America, at least–would feel comfortable with this manual, even with the accompanying translations to help them. In most institutions where Arabic is taught today, the first three years are oriented toward journalistic and simple modern belletristic prose, and only in his fourth year will the student, in most cases, be confronted by anything resembling a "classic". When given a cornucopia like the Beeston manual, he will either undergo a sense of deep discouragement and shock or painfully work his way through by leaning with all his weight on the translations. Some of this will obviously be necessary in any event, but overmuch dependence on the translations may well vitiate the usefulness of the work by not compelling the student to consult his reference grammar and dictionary as much as he should in order to seek out his own solutions. I think it would have been tactically better to put all the translations together in an appendix. The sheer tediousness of having to hunt down each word and line would act as a deterrent to overmuch consultation of the oracle. One can have so much prosthesis that the victim finds no need to walk!

The slight differences in the Arabic fonts used in printing the texts brought to mind an earlier collection of this type in which the very varied calligraphic styles reproduced were perhaps its most ingratiating and distinctive feature. I refer to the old *Mukhtārāt min al-Adab al-'Arabī* [An Arabic Chrestomathy for Advanced Students], American Council of Learned Societies, Washington, D.C., 1944, which was certainly a step on the right track, even if more than a few of the selections therein seemed rather idiosyncratic and injudiciously chosen. The fact is that in America, the student is more and more subjected, and limited, to reading the products of the Arabic typewriter and printer's *naskhī*, to the point that when he is shown anything else, it seems almost an alien and unfamiliar script. This is a misfortune, and some reader which would combine the best features of the *Mukhtārāt* and the Beeston manual is long overdue. Obviously, such a reader with translations accompanying the texts is directed more toward individual use than classroom instruction, but the fairly advanced student needs precisely such a bridge between his school texts and "real" books in Arabic, without vocabularies and notes in English. Before we have such a book, however, the present manual will serve admirably for individual self-instruction, provided the student restrains himself in the face of temptation.

One must cavil at something. On page 8, line 19, the dot should be removed from the *dāl* of *mina l-da 'a*. On page 9, lines 18 and 19 ought perhaps to be translated: "that such munificence as you divert to unworthy recipients will harm you by rendering you empty-handed before good men." On page 13, line 2, *šiddatu-hu* should be corrected to *šaddatu-hu*, as the Arabic text itself is vocalized. On page 39, lines 2 and 3, where 'brilliant magnificence' should be changed to 'the splendid [palace of] al-Zahrā.' And is not the usual vocalization of Al-Riḥānī's stage-name "Kiškiš"?

M. Lionel Bender and Hailu Fulass, *Amharic Verb Morphology* (Monograph No. 7, Committee on Ethiopian Studies). East Lansing, MI: African Studies Center, Michigan State University, 1978. Pp. xviii, 155.
By GROVER HUDSON, (Michigan State University)

This book is a transformational-generative grammar of Amharic verb morphology. The essence of the transformational-generative model of language description is explicitness through formalism (cf. Chomsky and Halle (1968: 331-32)). For morphology, this approach is based on precise claims about the underlying or lexical form of morphemes and how these are transformed by rules into words. This Bender and Hailu (B & H) have done for Amharic verbs, and it obviously wasn't easy. The study is a revision of Bender's 1968 Ph.D. dissertation. Hailu's contribution is apparent throughout, especially in the generative-semantic treatment of derived verbs (72-77) and an appendix consisting of a set of rules alternative to those derived from Bender 1968.

It is both refreshing and disturbing to see how the two authors have resolved their apparently frequent differences. Each author provides a preface; where the text reads 'I', we have material quoted from Bender 1968; 'we' means collaborative material; footnotes enable one author to take issue with a position of the other, which was accepted for the main text. This is refreshing, since in ignoring the usual desire for unanimity it recognizes controversial matters of language for what they are; it is disturbing, since it seems that a bit more time might have permitted the authors to agree to present differing opinions in a unified way and avoid selection of one or the other as the "main-text" opinion.

The haste in producing the study is apparent elsewhere, as will be discussed. The book's strength is a large number of tables and lists which illustrate what the transformational rules have to accomplish: the patterns of Amharic verb morphology. Once this is clear the actual statement of the formalized rules seems often a cryptographic exercise. The formalized rules will be of little use to most readers of the book, who will justifiably be uninterested in figuring out what they mean: these are persons interested mainly in Amharic. Persons interested in issues of linguistic theory and formal description I daresay will have trouble too, since B & H don't discuss how they are using some symbols, e.g. parentheses to mean "morpheme boundary", and they use others in unusual ways (angle-brackets on p. 36). They might well have followed the example of Schane (1968), whose transformational morphology of French totally avoided formalistic statement of rules.

Below I will take up each of the seven chapters of the book in order, plus the appendices, and for each make some general and specific comments.

1. First is an introductory chapter briefly reviewing the literature on Amharic, summarizing the familiar geolinguistic setting of the language and its sisters, and its classification. Prominent here is an extreme version of the traditional claim that Amharic, like all of Ethiopian Semitic, mixes Semitic and Cushitic-Omotic elements. "Extreme" is the reference to Amharic as a "creolized" or "post-creole" language (3-4). What Edward Sapir (1921: 206) said about the likelihood of mixed languages seems to me still relevant: "Language is probably the most self-contained, the most massively resistant of all social phenomena. It is easier to kill it off than to disintegrate its individual form." An apparent contradiction in this chapter probably reflects the authors' disagreement: we read that the argument "for a special Gurage link to the northern languages . . . is based on a few striking shared archaisms only", and yet "there is good reason to believe that they are the outgrowth of ancient military colonies from the north"(5). A missing reference in this section is Leslau (1965), the best means of access to studies on Amharic and all the Ethiopian Semitic languages. The comparative lexical study by Appleyard (1977) was probably unavailable to B & H, but he found in possible contrast to their claim that borrowed ("Cushomotic") words in the Amharic basic and cultural lexicon are "plentiful" (10), "a fairly high proportion of inherited Semitic material" (Appleyard 1977: 1).

2. Chapter 2 deals with the systematic phonemes of Amharic and their distinctive feature representation. B & H have chosen to retain the Jakobsonian distinctive features which were current at the time of Bender (1968). It is not entirely a matter of fashion that today these have been mostly replaced by the system of Chomsky and Halle (1968) or even more concrete systems such as that of Ladefoged (1975). The Jakobsonian features strive for a lot of economy, e.g. vowels and consonants are fully expressed by the same features, and tend to be somewhat arbitrary in assignment. In B & H's distinctive feature matrix (13) the glottal stop (which they present as a phoneme although it has often been considered a phonetic effect of Amharic vowel sequences, e.g. /säat/ 'hour' = [säʔat]) is not a stop but a glide; /r/ is said to be [+high] and /l/ [-high] (apparently as a way to make these two distinct); inexplicably, labial and dental consonants are said to be [+low], with the exception of /r/, and the Amharic affricates are termed non-strident.

B & H need the feature "flat" in consonants to express those verbs which have the vowel /o/

after a radical consonant: the lexically flat consonants are labialized and are transformed into a consonant followed by /o/: *m^w^äla* → *mola* 'fill (vi)'; the feature "sharp" plays the same role in providing the vowel /e/ or consonant palatalization: *t'^y^äsä* → *t'esä* / *c'äsä* 'smoke (vi)' (they say that dialects with C^w will get this from C*o* by low-level rules" (51)). They discuss the possibility that the vowel /ɨ/ might be omitted from Amharic underlying representations, but reject this on the grounds that /ɨ/ is contrastive in pairs like *sɨm* 'name' vs. *säm* 'wax'. They refer to Hetzron (1964), who, while he seemed to conclude in favor of the elimination of /ɨ/, noted that this was only possible with the provision of a phoneme of "juncture" /-/ to assure, for example, a pronunciation [ɨbd] 'crazy' from /-bd/; /bd/ would be ambiguous. This raises the possibility that the phonemic glottal stop could provide the disambiguating environment: /ʔbd/ would have to be pronounced [ʔɨbd]. The argument that /ɨ/ contrasts with the other vowels in cases like *sam* / *säm* is tautological: if there is no distinctive /ɨ/, the contrast is of *sm* vs. *säm*, a vowelless vs. vowelled word.

3. The third chapter presents their scheme of Amharic verb types. B & H accept the idealization of Semitic "root and pattern morphology" that lexical verbs consist of consonants only, with all vocalization provided by phonological and morphological rules. This is descriptively possible since the aforementioned labialized and palatalized consonants provide for occurrences of stem-vowels /o/ and /e/, respectively, and setting up the radical consonant /h/ provides occurrences of stem-vowel /a/. This of course is a rough mirror of the historical facts, though other back consonants than /h/ yielded /a/, and the origin of the vowel /e/ of the B-type verbs is obscure. The main question to ask is what if anything is gained by this descriptive procedure. Certainly there are generalizations about Amharic derivable in this way: just those which the historical processes have put into the language through vowel-lowerings, delabializations, and palatalizations. But, as B & H's Table 3 (24-25) shows, for every "abstract" or fictive consonant introduced into lexical entries, there is a vowelled ACTUAL form. Clearly, introducing these vowels into lexical entries would eliminate the need for the rules to derive them. But it remains to show, against B & H, that the generalization of all-consonantal roots, thereby lost, does not have the significance which they claim for it (45-46; simplification of rules and derivations is not claimed).

4. Chapter 4 deals with phonological redundancies abstractable from the lexical entries of verbs, for example, the statement that these take the shape C_2^5 (30), i.e. no more than five nor fewer than two consonants. The notations "I(C)" and "T(C)" in these rules, by the way, stand for "If (Condition)" and "Then (Condition)". The significance of these rules ranges from the universal (no. 318: all obstruents are consonantal and non-nasal); to the probably accidental (no. 13: there are no flat (labialized) final consonants).

Rule 12 is puzzling. It implies that gemination is redundant in triradicals verbs, when the authors also state here that it is this feature in C_2 of triradicals which differentiates the A and B-type verbs (cf. also p. 46). Rule 14, which requires that any pair of obsruents in a verb root be either identical or non-homorganic, B & H consider to require controversial (extrinsic) disjunctive ordering of the two parts, which they say are "contradictory" (31). This concern seems unnecessary: since the rule does not change any features but just expresses a redundancy in, or necessity for, verbs, there is no contradiction; the parts constitute a simple either/or statement.

Rule 311 says "continuant obstruents . . . are the only strident segments"; all others are non-strident (35). But it is analytically true that only obstruents can be strident, so the statement that non-obstruents are non-strident need not be a part of the grammar of any language. What B & H want to say here is that in Amharic there are no non-strident fricatives: I(C) [+obstruent, +continuant]; T(C) [+strident]. The use of angle-brackets in their Rule 311 seems to me unprecedented (as also in Rule 316). One other example to show the confusion inherent in strict formalization: MSC 319 (36) they interpret "*f* is voiceless", a tautology. What they mean to say is "the labial fricative is voiceless (there is no *v*)".

5. This chapter presents the main rules for forming the different stem-types: perfect, contingent (imperfect), gerund, jussive, and infinitive. B & H present (53-61) a long and careful table showing how the twelve rules of this chapter affect each underlying verb type. The first step, Rule 2 (Rule 1 finds no environments of application until after Rule 4), is to convert root *h*'s to *a*. So it is apparent that there can be no usefulness in derivations in positing these *h*'s; their ONLY purpose is to permit the necessarily hypothetical generalization that verb roots are vowelless. Rule 3 is said to geminate penultimate consonants (unless already geminate lexically, i.e. B-type) in the perfect and, if quadriradical, in the contingent. Actually, what the formal notation implies is that the penultimate SEGMENT, vowel or consonant, is geminated, so B & H's claim (47) that a stem *lak* 'send' (once removed from lexical *lhk*) is out of the scope of the rule can only be true if we assume that their morpheme structure condition 313 (35) (vowels are [-geminate]) blocks gemination. It is subtleties of interpretation like this that will, I am sure, make it next to impossible for most readers to believe that these rules work. Or consider Rule 4, which is supposed to insert the first order vowel *ä* after all but the final consonant of roots (48): $X [\ ] [\ ] Y)_v \rightarrow X [\ ]\, \ddot{a}\, [\ ] Y)_v$. It is stated that X and Y may not be zero, a condition said to prevent application of the rule on a biradical root such as *š*^{w}*m* 'appoint'. But now bi- OR triradical roots are unaffected by the rule, which in order to apply requires FOUR segments at least. Perhaps they wanted to say that only Y may not be zero, but on this interpretation the rule will never insert *ä* after a penultimate consonant, since TWO segments are required AFTER the place of insertion.

There are references on p. 48 to two rules which are never presented: "degemination" and "resyllabification". Rule A (63) for deriving agents, ought to use square rather than curly brackets, in order to associate the two alternatives in S.D. and S.C. In rule R (63), the square brackets on item 3 should be omitted and the curly brackets expanded to indicate the alternatives [+syllabic], [-low] C, and [+low]. Rule T1 (64) is an interesting positive example of how the explicitness of formalism may clarify some synchronic processes. An intrusive stem-final *t* in gerundive and infinitive forms of some apparent biradicals, e.g. *sämt-*, *-smat* 'hear', is seen by this rule to replace a final vowel in the gerundive (converb) and to be suffixed in the infinitive, exactly as it should if in fact it is functioning like a historical radical consonant (cf. for 'break', *säbr-*, *-sbär*).

6. Chapter 6 deals with the derived stems with the causative and passive prefixes. There is a discussion of the correlation of A and B-type with transitivity and of the latter with the acceptance of a verb of the causative (*a-* and *as-*) and reflexive-passive (*tä-*) prefixes. B & H find some statistical evidence of significance for the correlation of A-type and intransitive and B-type and transitive. Again they present useful tables and lists showing the patterns of stem-

changes with the prefixes. There are three good sources touching on these topics which might have been mentioned: Hetzron (1963), Cowley (1969), and Gragg (1970).

They propose a sort of "generative semantics" (as opposed to "lexicalist") approach by which the prefixed verbs result from reduction of complex sentences in which the prefixes function as abstract, "higher" verbs. I am puzzled by some aspects of the underlying tree structures they present, for example, what role the first *wɨha* 'water' plays in their deep structure for *lɨǰ wɨha afälla* "the boy boiled water' (sic): [$_S$ lɨǰ [$_{VP}$ wɨha [$_S$ wɨha fälla $_S$] a$_V$ $_{VP}$] $_S$] (74). A more usual conception would be that what is "caused" by the abstract verb *a* in this sentence is the simple sentence *wɨha fälla.*

B & H remind us of the interesting fact that reflexive-passive prefix *t-* (their underlying *tä-*) is absent where it is compounded with *-n-* and *-š-* in the tenses with subject prefixes. The at least historical independence of the *-n-* and *-š-* is indeed indicated by this fact (cf. *tän-bäräkkäkä* vs. *yɨn-bäräkkäk* "kneel', *täš-k'ädaddämä* vs. *yɨ-š-k'ädaddäm* 'race (vi)'), but the 'disappearance' of *t-* in these environments does not show the necessity for its transformational deletion (or a non-transformational zero-allomorph of this prefix, as in Hudson (1978); suggested by B & H, p. 87). Rather, synchronically speaking, we can suppose that *-t-* is just not inserted in these environments. Historically, it seems reasonable that these are relic environments, where because of the presence of the subject prefix, secondary, reflexive *t-* could not be generalized from other verbs where it was spreading at the expense and eventually to the virtual replacement of passive *n-*.

7. Chapter 7 presents the rules for generating derived stems, as modifications of the rules for basic stems. Table 8 (89) nicely shows what modifications are required. B & H suggest (90) that the fact that all stems with the *as-* causative prefix are B-types (with geminate second consonant) is due to some characteristic of 'weight' in this prefix. Again, a historical understanding may be adequate for this fact (if no less speculative at this time), here the hypothesis that in origin (*a*)*s-* combined only with B-type stems, which were transitive (Hudson 1979). One of their claims about the facts is news to me: that the second consonant of A-type passive triradical stems is optionally geminated in the agent (Rule A, 93), e.g. *täsäbbari* 'broken one' is possible.

Readers will find puzzlement about some of the rules in this chapter too. The modification of Rule 3 (93) seems confused. They add the specification [+consonantal] to the medial radical consonant "to block application for *h* in Class 7 verbs". But as they mentioned in the discussion of original Rule 3 (47-48), Rule 2 ($h \rightarrow a$) has already accomplished this by removing *h*'s from the scene. Furthermore, the specification [+consonantal] will also exclude medial glides *w* and *y*, so the rule will now fail in the cases of numerous derived verbs like *as-awwäk'ä* 'quaint' and *tä-däwwälä* 'be rung'. Rule T (95) should again use square instead of curly brackets in order to properly associate the gemination of *t* of the prefix with *a*-initial verbs, and its deletion and consequent gemination of a stem-initial consonant with presence of the latter. Also, since Rule T has an undefined variable as item 8 of S.D., item 9 could not be identified in order to be affected by the rule.

8. Finally, there are several appendices: a set of alternative rules (developed by Hailu) for basic and derived stems but I think presented too cursorily to warrant close examination,

e.g. Rule Pa2, p. 97, inserts an undefined V and apparently deletes an undefined X; a lexicon of 1277 Amharic verb roots arranged in classes (an alphabetical list would have been more useful), each glossed, marked as transitive, intransitive or impersonal, and classified as to which prefixes it accepts; a list of "representative verbs," which appears to add little or nothing to the exhaustive list; and a list of verbs which remain exceptions to the rules presented, with discussion of these.

This is a book that needed to be written, and I'm sure the authors must look upon the effort as more or less experimental. They have provided the basis for a great deal of necessary work on the transformational, explicit grammar of Amharic verb morphology. To some extent the book's shortcomings of formal notation are due to the immature notation system itself. And the discussion, lists, tables, and charts of the book are more valuable than the formalized rules anyway. I see amazingly few typographical errors, and only three noteworthy composition errors: p. 37, instead of "only round varieties of g, k . . . ", "round varieties of only g, k . . . "; p. 43, the perfect stems of 1c and 2c type verbs ought to be geminated (*näggʷäd-*, *čäkkʷäl-*); and p. 88, "Agents of A-type verbs" (not "vowels").

References

APPLEYARD, D. L.
1977 "A comparative approach to the Amharic lexicon." Afroasiatic Linguistics 5/2: 1-67.

BENDER, M. L.
1968 "Amharic verb morphology: a generative approach." Ph.D. dissertation, University of Texas at Austin.

CHOMSKY, N. and M. Halle
1968 *The Sound Pattern of English*. New York: Harper and Row.

COWLEY, R.
1969 "A and B verbal stem type in Amharic." *Journal of Ethiopian Studies* 7: 1-13.

GRAGG, G. B.
1970 "Overt and covert categories in derivational morphology." *Papers from the Sixth Regional Meeting, Chicago Linguistic Society*, pp. 262-69. Chicago: CLS.

HETZRON, R.
1963 "La rection du thème factitif en amharique." *Le Muséon* 76: 425-39.
1964 "La voyelle du sixième ordre en amharique." Journal of African Languages 3: 179-90.

HUDSON, G.
1978 "Lexical form of the Amharic reflexive-passive." *Para Session on the Lexicon*, pp. 210-219. Chicago: CLS.
1979 "The Ethiopian Semitic B-type." In D. Levine et al. (eds.), *Proceedings of the Fifth International Conference on Ethiopian Studies, pp. 101-110.* Chicago: University of Illinois at Chicago Circle.

LADEFOGED, P.
1975. *A Course in Phonetics*. New York: Harcourt Brace.

LESLAU, W.
1965 *An Annotated Bibliography of the Semitic Languages of Ethiopia.* The Hague: Mouton.

SAPIR, E.
1921 *Language.* New York: Harcourt Brace (Harvest Book ed.).

SCHANE, S.
1968 *French Phonology and Morphology.* Cambridge, Mass.: MIT Press.

T. M. Johnstone, *Ḥarsūsi Lexicon and English-Ḥarsūsi Word-List.* London: Oxford University Press, 1977. 211 pp.
by RICHARD C. STEINER (Yeshiva University, New York)

The Ḥarsūsi language is so important to Semitists and so close to extinction, and our knowledge of it so meager and so imperfect, that a new lexicon of that language cannot fail to be an important contribution to the field of Semitics. Every one of us in this field owes the author a debt of gratitude for undertaking this task.

The *Ḥarsūsi lexicon* (henceforth ḤL) begins with a combined preface-and-acknowledgements (v-vi) followed by an introduction (ix-xxvi). Distributed between these two sections is much valuable new information about the Ḥarāsīs (the final *s* in this form is NOT the English plural morpheme!) and their language. The sociolinguistic tidbits are fresh and interesting. The author makes good use of his knowledge of Omani Arabic in describing the intimate relationships between that language and Ḥarsūsi in the daily life of this bilingual tribe.

Also included in the introduction are phonological notes which supply a wealth of phonetic, morphophonemic, phonotactic, and historical information about the vowels and selected consonants of Ḥarsūsi and the other MSA languages. These notes, as well as certain other features of this work, remind one inevitably of its illustrious predecessor, Leslau's *Lexique Soqoṭri.*

It is interesting to compare Johnstone's phonological data with those of earlier writers. Johnstone writes (p. xiii) that "*śl* occurs quite frequently as a variant of *ś*" in Ḥarsūsi and Socotri (henceforth Ḥ and S), whereas "this is quite rare in Mehri and Śḥeri" (henceforth M and Ś). Carter (1847: 343), on the other hand, gives the impression that this phenomenon is quite common in Mehri:

> ش has a very peculiar sound in the Mahra dialect; it is formed by placing the tip of the tongue against the anterior part of the palate, and allowing the air to pass out of the mouth on one side or the other of it, in the manner of a lisp, following it with the sound of the letter *l* as in شيوط "fire" pronounced *shleeote.*

It is, of course, possible that Carter's generalization is based on only one example, but it is equally possible that we are dealing here with diachronic change or dialectal variation (the southwestern dialect of *bilād Mahra* recorded by Carter vs. the northeastern dialect of Dhofar recorded by Johnstone).

The phenomenon discussed above is similar to one in Hein's Mehri texts pointed out by Bittner (1910:81): "Für die Artikulation des *ś* bezeichnend ist es, dass Hein statt *ś* etlichemale *lś* schreibt . . . " This variant of *ś* (*lś* rather than *śl*) is reported by Johnstone for Welsh but not for Modern South Arabian (henceforth MSA).

Before leaving this point, I might remark that Johnstone's presentation of it is puzzling. He begins by stating that "the lateral fricative *ś* is unlike the Welsh *ll* in that in essence it has no *l*-glide. The Welsh *ll* in other words could be transcribed *śl* or *lś* in terms of the Ḥ consonant system." But then he does an about-face, stating that "it is a fact, however, that in Ḥ (and in Socotri) *śl* occurs quite frequently as a variant of *ś* . . . " Is this merely a roundabout way of saying that Welsh *ll* always has an *l*-glide while Ḥ and S have it only "quite frequently"? If so, Johnstone's perception of Welsh *ll* clashes quite sharply with that of Rositzke (1939:8).

A more important difference between Johnstone and his predecessors concerns palatalization in Ś. Fresnel (1838:538, 544, 545), Bittner (1916:19-20 and 1917 s.v.) and Thomas (1937 s.v.) usually transcribe the palatalized alternants of the velar stops as affricates, while Johnstone transcribes them as fricatives,[1] as shown in the following chart:

	Fresnel[2]	Bittner	Thomas	Johnstone
'scorpion'	*t̲t̲c̲h̲în,* *t̲s̲s̲în*	––	*ic̲h̲i'in* (M *q̱ubãin*)	*ṣ̌ 'īn* (Ḥ̱M *ḵebáyn*)
'to drink' (Sem *šḵ̣y*)	*schout̲s̲s̲i*	––	*shid̲z̲ī*	*šúṣ̌i*
'coast, beach' (Eth *ḥäyḵ̣*)	––	*ḥayč̱*	*ḥaic̲h̲, ḥut̲z̲* (M *ḥaiḵ*)	*ḥayṣ̌* (M *ḥayḵ̣*)
'town' (Sem *ḵ̣aryat-*)	––	*č̱irét*	*iẕīret*	*ṣ̌'irɛt*[3]
'you two'	*-t̲s̲î*	––	––	*-š̱i* (ḤMS *-ḵi*)
'(riding) camels' (Sem *rḵb*)	––	*arč̱ób,* *erč̱ób*	*urt̲s̲op*	*rš̱ɔb*[3] (M *rīḵōb*)[3]
'young she-camels' (Sem *baḵrat-*)	––	*beč̱órten*	––	–– (ḤM *beḵōr*)
'to skin'	––	*dḥaš̱*	––	*dḥáš* (ḤM *deḥāḵ*)

[1] In a letter received shortly before completion of this review, Johnstone assures me that they are indeed fricatives. As for Johnstone (1975b), where the palatalized allophone of *k* is given as ᵗʃ' (= ᵗš̃'), Johnstone writes that he has always been a little uneasy about the Ś dialect dealt with in that note, because it was the second language of a Mehri speaker (of the Eastern dialect).

[2] From the discussion on pp. 538, 544, and 545 (cf. pp. 543-4), it is clear that the sounds which which Fresnel (1938) writes *ttch, tss, ts, dz,* and *dj* are all PALATAL affricates. I presume that the signs s̃, z̃, and ṣ̃ (used by Johnstone in his letter to me) also indicate palatal articulation.

[3] From Johnstone (1975a:7-8) rather than ḤL.

'two men'	*ghod̲z̲î*	*ġuġ-i* [*ġ=j*]	––	*ɣuž̲i*, *ɣɔž̲i*[3] (M *ɣawgi*)[3]
'vein, sinew, root' (Sem *g̲īd-*)	––	*ġ̲iód*	––	*ž̲id*
'female slave'	––	*ġ̲irít*	*ī̲jirit* (M *hag̲irīt*)	*ž̲írét* (ḤM *ḥāg̲erēt*)
'eyebrows'	*hhid̲j̲ol*	––	––	–– (M *ḥeg̲éwwel*)

In view of the well-known tendency of palatalization and affrication to be followed by assibilation, the most likely explanation for this difference between Johnstone and his predecessors would seem to be historical change.

It is worth noting that there are two cases in which a majority of the older sources agree with Johnstone in giving a sibilant rather than an affricate as the palatalized reflex of *k*:

'liver' (Sem *k̲abid-*)	––	*š̲ibdít*	*s̲ubdait*	*š̲ubdét*
'you(r) (f.s.)' (Sem *-k̲i*)	*-(é)c̲h̲* [*ch=ç*]	*-š̲*	––	*-š̲*

Now it so happens that these lexical items also contain a sibilant in Ḥ & M (where evidence of palatalization is rare) and in S. It seems possible, therefore, that there are two layers of palatalization in Ś: a proto-MSA layer represented by *šubdét* and *-š*, which reached the sibilant stage long ago, and a distinctively Ś layer, which, for most lexical items, reached the sibilant stage only recently, in the last 50 years.

Whether or not this hypothesis is correct, one thing is clear: the form *-š* 'your (f.s.)' is a very old one. In fact, it is mentioned already by Mas'ūdī (1861:333) in the tenth century:

> wa-'ahlu š-Šiḥr 'unās min Quḍā'ah ibn Mālik ibn Ḥimyar wa-ġayrihim mina l-'arab wa-yud'ā man sakana hād̲ā l-balad mina l-'arabi l-Mahrah . . . wa-luġatuhum bi-xilāf luġati l-'arab wa-d̲ālika 'annahum yaj'alūna š-šin badalan mina l-kāf wa-mit̲la d̲ālika qawluhum hel leš fīmā qult(i?) lī wa-qult leš 'en tej'al (masc.!)[4] l-led̲ī ma'ī fī l-led̲ī ma'eš . . .
>
> [And the folk of Shiḥr[5] are people descended from Quḍā'ah son of Mālik son of Ḥimyar and other Arabs. And those Arabs who inhabit this country are called Mahrah . . . and their language is different from the language of the Arabs in that they put *š* in exchange for *k* and say, for example, 'Do you have (*leš* for *lek*) control over the matter you discussed with me?' and 'I told you (*leš* for *lek*) to put that which is with me with that which is with you (*ma'eš* for *ma'ek*)' . . .]

[4] This form, if original, indicates that Mas'ūdī mistakenly believed *-š* to be a MASCULINE pronoun.

[5] The country of Shiḥr referred to in this passage is not the home of the Ṣheri (or, at least, not their present-day home in the mountains of Dhofar) but rather an area of Ḥaḍramut (cf. Mas'ūdī 1865:12,14). It is the place called *Scier* by Marco Polo and *Shi-ho* by Chau Ju-Kua.

Finally, we might compare Johnstone's description of the MSA emphatics with the descriptions of his predecessors. Most of the latter were not aware that these consonants are glottalic, but Fresnel certainly was. He reports (1838:545) that the Ś emphatics

> exigent un certain gonflement des amygdales, et sont, pour ainsi dire, CRACHÉES par une émission violente et subite de l'air comprimé dans le larnyx. Le *ssad* ص peut etre représenté (conventionellement) par *ss*, le ص̣ par *ttch* ou *tss*, le ط par *tt*, le ظ par *tth* et le ق par *ck*; mais, à moins d'avoir ouï parler l'amharique (*amara* ou éthiopien moderne, on ne peut deviner ce que j'entends ici par *tt* ou *ck*.

This report has been ignored by all twentieth-century scholars with the exception of Yushmanov (1930:383-4). Johnstone deserves credit for his independent confirmation of Fresnel's discovery and for pointing out that the MSA emphatics all have voiced "pre-glottalized" allophones alongside the voiceless ejective ones.

Unfortunately, "pre-glottalized" is an ambiguous term. It properly refers to a sound produced during its initial phase with a CLOSED and STATIONARY glottis, but I have also seen it used as a synonym of "implosive", i.e. a sound in which voicing is produced, according to Catford (1977:74-7), by the upward leak of air through an OPEN, downward-MOVING glottis. No doubt the two types are difficult to distinguish and phonologically related (Greenberg 1970:124-5); nevertheless, more exact information (in some future publication) would be of great value.

Of particular interest is the fact that, according to Johnstone, the basic allophone of *ṣ/ẓ* and *ṭ/ḍ* is voiceless, as is *ḳ*, whereas the basic allophone of *ḏ̣/ṯ̣* is voiced. It is striking that, despite the many differences between the emphatics of MSA and those of classical Arabic, the basic allophones of the MSA emphatics are identical to their Arabic counterparts (*ṣ, ṭ, q,* and *ḏ̣*) with regard to voicing.

We come now to the lexicon itself (pp. 1-181). This is a fine piece of work which combines most of the advantages of its predecessors. Like *Lexique Soqoṭri* it gives cognates from other MSA languages (so that proto-forms can be reconstructed) and Omani Arabic (so that borrowings can be eliminated), and it has an index in which the glosses became lemmas (pp. 153-81). Like Thomas' quadrilingual word-lists (the only other source for Ḥ), it records the perceptions of only one ear (so that precise comparison is possible), it gives semantic equivalents which are not cognates (so that comparative onomasiological studies can be undertaken), and it includes all but one of the five MSA languages. Finally, it surpasses both of the above in accuracy and completeness.

The importance of ḤL for comparative Semitic lexicography will be obvious to anyone who opens it. It contains, by my count, at least 290 conservative cognates of Hebrew lexical items. It is true that most of these cognates do not add much to what has long been known from Arabic (a language, which is equally archaic from a phonological, if not phonetic, point of view), but more than a few of them do, either because the Arabic cognate in question has changed its meaning or because it has totally disappeared. I have found twenty such cognates in ḤL, of which only nine are discussed by Leslau (1958). The following notes deal with some of those twenty and a number of other MSA lexical items from ḤL and earlier works which should be of interest to Semitic lexicographers:

1) ḤM *'ād* < **'ād* 'still, yet, again' = Hebrew *'oδ* , Ethiopic *'adi* 'still, yet, again'.

2) Ḥ *fēn*, M *fenw-*, Ś *fín-* 'before, in front of' = Hebrew *lifne*, Ugaritic *lpn* 'before, in front of'.

3) ḤM *egtemōl* 'to be generous, treat well' = Hebrew *gåmal*, Aramaic *gmal*, Akkadian *ǧamālu* 'mete out (good/bad)'. MSA shows an intermediate stage of the semantic change which resulted in Arabic *ǧamula* 'be beautiful'.

4) ḤM *ġōreb*, Ś *ġarb*, S *'areb* < **ġareb* 'base of neck, part of camel's neck in front of the hump' = Akkadian *arūbu* 'a part of the neck', Hebrew *'orεf* 'back of neck' = Arabic *'urf* 'mane (of horse)'. The two halves of this equation are not necessarily mutually exclusive, since *ġ*/ ' fluctuation in the vicinity of *r* is common in South Semitic (Steiner 1977:135).

5) ḤM *šīt*, Ś *šet*, S *šeh* 'backside, posterior' (e.g. *yezḥáyfem le-štōtihem* 'they shuffled along on their backsides') = Hebrew *šeθ* (e.g. *'aδ šəθoθehεm* 'until their buttocks', II Sam. 10:4), Arabic *ist* 'backside, buttocks'.

6) Ḥ *źōfa'*, M *źōfeġ*, S *źofġ* 'cattle dung' = Hebrew *ṣəfi'e båḳår* 'cattle dung', Ethiopic *ḍəfə'* 'excrement (human or animal)'.

7) ḤM *kenemōt*, Ś *šinit* < **knmt*, S *kanum* 'louse' = Hebrew *kinnåm*, Aramaic *ḳ/kalm-*, *ḳml*, Arabic *qaml*, ESA *ḳmlt*, Ethiopic *ḳʷəmal*, Akkadian *kalmatu* 'lice/louse'. The MSA languages are the only ones which have a cognate whose consonants correspond normally with those of the Hebrew form.

8) Ḥ *neṯōk*, M *neṯk* 'to bite' = Hebrew *nåšax*, Ugaritic *nṯk*, Aramaic *nxe/aθ*, Akkadian *našāku*, Ethiopic *näsäkä* 'to bite'.

9) Ḥ *mešxáwt*, M *xōt* < **hxōt* < **šxōt*, Ś *šxot* (Bittner 1917: *enšḥót*), S *šḥoh* < **šxoh* 'armpit' = Mishnaic Hebrew *šεḥi*, Aramaic *šiḥyå*, *šḥåθå* 'armpit'. The occurence of *x* in the MSA forms strengthens the connection of the Hebrew and Aramaic forms with Akkadian *šaḫātu* 'side', but precludes any connection between them and the root *šḥy* 'bend' if the latter is related at all to Hebrew *yištaḥăwε*, Ugaritic *yštḥwy* 'bow down'. Perhaps they are related (distantly) to Hebrew *šu/iḥå*, *šaḥaθ* 'pit', Mari Akkadian (< Amorite) *saxatum* 'pitfall' (Pardee 1978:93fn), Akkadian *ḫaštu* 'pit', and Arabic *sāxa* 'sink (in mud)'.

10) ḤM *ḥelīt*, Ś *ḥálét* 'rust' = Hebrew *ḥεl'å* 'rust'. Leslau (1958) has only one MSA cognate: S *ḥal'eh* 'dirt'.

11) Ḥ *yōda*, M *wēda*, Ś *éda'*, S *eda'* 'to know' = Hebrew *yåδa'*, Ugaritic *yd'*, Aramaic *yδa'*, Akkadian *e/idū*, *wadū*, ESA *yd'*, etc. 'to know'. It is not clear whether to reconstruct *w* or *y* as the initial consonant of the Proto-Semitic root. Leslau (1958) has the M form but not the Ḥ form, thus giving the impression that MSA supports Akkadian *wadū* against ESA *yd'*, Ethiopic *'äydə'ä*, and Arabic *'ayda'a*.

12) ḤM *'āfōr*, Ś *'áfór* 'cloud; dust wind'. Could this be a blend of Hebrew *'årif*, Ugaritic *'rpt*, Akkadian *urpu* 'cloud(s)' and Hebrew *'åfår*, Ugaritic *'pr*, Akkadian *ep(e)ru* 'dust'?

13) Ḥ *fām*, M *fēm*, Ś *fa'm* 'foot, leg' = Hebrew *pa'am*, Phoenician *p'm* 'foot; time', Akkadian *pēm/nu* 'thigh'. Gordon's theory (1965:466) that the Hebrew-Phoenician form is a blend of *p'm* 'time' and *p'n* 'foot' (the forms attested in Ugaritic) is weakened somewhat by the final *m* in the MSA forms listed above.

14) ḤM *śẽf* 'trace, track; footprint; foot', Ś *śέf* 'track, trace', S *śab*, S (Qádub) *śaf* 'foot' = Akkadian *šēpu* 'foot'. Von Soden (1959) s.v. *šēpu* gives the West-Semitic equivalents of *šēpu* as 'rigl usw', overlooking the Akkadian-Socotri correspondence noted already, according to Leslau (1938:424), by Halévy in REVUE SÉMITIQUE, July 1905. ḤL confirms Halevy's insight by showing that the other MSA languages and one dialect of S have an *f* < **p* rather than a *b* in this word. Indeed, even in "standard" S, the dual form of this word (*śáfi, śa'fi*) has an *f* (Leslau 1938:424). It is now clear that this *f* did not develop from *b* via a conditioned sound change, as Leslau (1938:424) believed, but rather came from **p* via the well-known unconditional South Semitic sound change.

15) ḤM *ḏebēr*, Ś *εḏbir*, S *édbehir* < **éḏbehir* 'hornet, bee' = Hebrew *dǝvorå̄* 'bee', Aramaic *zabbur(iθ)å̄, debbor(t)å̄*, etc., 'bee, wasp', Arabic *zunbūr, dabbūr* 'hornet'. The MSA evidence makes a confusing situation even worse. Eilers' suggestion (1971:585, 598) that Arabic *zunbūr* is a borrowing of Iranian **zanba'bar* < *zamb* "Kampf" would clear things up a bit, if only it were plausible.

16) Ś *reś* 'to crawl (ants)', M *riśś* 'to crawl (spider)' (Jahn 1902), *amriś* 'to crawl' (Thomas 1937) = Hebrew *rå̄maś* 'to crawl, creep'. The deletion of *m* is usual in Ś but not in M.

17) ḤMŚ *ḥamṯ*, S *ḥant* < **ḥanṯ* 'lower belly, pubes' = Hebrew *ḥomεš* 'a vital spot or organ in the body', Ethiopic *ḥǝmš* 'uterus', Tigre *ḥǝms* 'pubes, abdomen', Akkadian *em/nsu* 'hypogastric region'. This correspondence is noted by Johnstone himself in ḤL. Prior to the publication of ḤL, the S form was thought to be connected with Tigre *ḥanot* 'foetus' (Leslau 1938). Conversely, the Hebrew, Akkadian, and Ethiopic forms listed above were thought to contain an etymological **š*, in view of Syriac *ḥumšå̄*. Johnstone's note prompted Degen (1978) to take a closer look at that Syriac form. An examination of the internal Syriac evidence showed that *ḥumšå̄* is a borrowing from Hebrew.

18) Ś *fizḥait* 'forehead' (Thomas 1937). This form shows that Hebrew *meṣaḥ* 'forehead' is etymologically related to Jewish Aramaic (> Mishnaic Hebrew) *paddaḥtå̄* 'forehead' (and Ethiopic *fǝṣǝm* 'forehead'?), and that Jewish Aramaic *miṣḥå̄* 'forehead', for which only one source is given by Jastrow (1950 s.v.), is a Hebraism. The correspondence between Hebrew *ṣ* and Aramaic *d* is attested elsewhere (Hebrew *pεṣa'* 'wound' = Aramaic *piδ'å̄*, 'wound') and is easily explained as coming from one of two normal correspondences: Hebrew *z* = Aramaic *d* or Hebrew *ṣ* = Aramaic *ṭ*. The former correspondence leads us to MSA *ḏ*, the latter to MSA *ḏ̣*. Both of these are normally written *dh* by Thomas, but the latter appears at least once (s.v. *noon*) as *z*. I hope that Johnstone will be able to give a definitive answer to this question in some future publication.

19) Ś *le* 'cow' (Thomas 1937) = Akkadian *lū* 'bull', *littu, lītu* 'cow', Arabic *la'ātu* 'wild cow', Hebrew *Le'å̄* 'Leah' (sister of *Rå̄ḥel* 'Rachel; ewe'). Schuh (1979:256) mistakenly connects Southern Cushitic **ɬee-* 'cow' and Chadic **ɬa* 'cow' with Akkadian *šū, šu'u* 'sheep', Arabic *šāh* 'sheep, ewe', Hebrew *śε* and Ugaritic *š* 'sheep, goat' instead of the above words for 'cow'.

20) a) singular ḤMS *ber*, Ś *bεr* 'son' = Aramaic *bar* < *bir* 'son', but plural ḤM *ḥe-būn*, Ś *īn* 'sons' = Aramaic *bnin* 'sons'.

b) singular ḤM *bert*, S *ebret-* 'daughter' = Aramaic *braθ* 'daughter', but plural Ḥ *ḥe-bōnten*, M *ḥe-bánten*, Ś *ōnte* 'daughters' = Aramaic *bnå̄n*, *bnå̄θå̄* 'daughters'.

c) cardinal ḤM *ṯerō*, Ś *ṯro*, S *tra* 'two' = Aramaic *tren* 'two' but ordinal Ḥ *ṯēni*, M *ṯōni* 'second' = Aramaic *tinyå̄n* 'second' (although these ordinal forms are not entirely comparable).

It is striking that MSA and Aramaic, against all of the other Semitic languages,[6] have an *r* in the words for 'son', 'daughter', and 'two',[7] and when the alternation with *n* is taken into account, the similarity becomes astounding. No wonder Christian (1944) was convinced that MSA and Aramaic are closely related! Scholars who reject this view, and that includes just about everyone, must project this alternation back into Proto-(West-)Semitic.

It is worth noting that the two morphemes involved here have something else in common: their Arabic forms, *ibn(at)un* and *iṯn(at)āni*, have a base consisting of two consonants WITH NO VOWEL IN BETWEEN. A similar form must be reconstructed as the ancestor of the much-discussed Hebrew *štayim* 'two (f.).' The latter can hardly be the reflex of **ṯintaym* since vowels in closed syllables are immune to deletion in Hebrew. It is more reasonable to posit an original **ṯn̥taym* or **iṯn̥taym*, with a syllabic *n̥*, which yielded **(i)šttayim* and then *(i)štayim*. If so, it is conceivable that *r* alternated with *n* in Proto-(West-)Semitic in positions where a syllabic consonant was called for, e.g. *tn̥taym* ~ *tr̥taym, bn̥tum* ~ *br̥tum*, but not where *n* was non-syllabic, e.g. *banātum* 'daughters'. But this is just a guess, and not a very convincing one, at that.

21) Ḥ *'arḳáyb ḏe-fām* 'Achilles' tendon' = Arabic *'urqūb* 'Achilles' tendon, hamstring, hock', Syriac *'arḳubba*[8] 'Achilles' tendon, ham (popliteal space)', Mishnaic Hebrew *'arḳov* 'hock', and, according to (Wajnberg 1935:57), Tigre *tärḳub* 'hock'. The literal meaning of the Ḥ expression is 'mouse of the leg'.

This figure of speech reminds one inevitably of Old French *soriz* which means both 'mouse' and 'calf of the leg' and of the many other Indo-European words which mean both 'mouse' and 'muscle': Greek μῦς, Latin *musculus*, Old Norse, Old High German, and Old English *mūs*, Dutch *muis*. Indeed the Syriac cognate of Ḥ *'arḳáyb*, M *'ārḳáyb*, S *'arḳéb* 'mouse' is *'uḳbrå*, whose feminine form means both 'female mouse' and 'muscle', although this may be a loan-translation from Greek.[9]

Did the connection between 'mouse' and 'Achilles' tendon' exist already in Proto-Semitic or is this an MSA innovation? To answer this question, we must examine the cognates of *'arḳáyb* in the other Semitic languages, e.g. Akkadian *akbaru* 'jerboa?', *arrabu* 'dormouse?, jerboa?' (both from OB), Syriac *'uḳbrå* 'mouse, jerboa', Hebrew *'axbår* 'mouse, jerboa', Arabic *'akābir* 'mice, jerboas', Tigre *'ekrib* 'badger'. These forms do not lend a great deal of support to the notion that the Proto-Semitic word for 'mouse' agreed with the MSA word in having an

---

[6] Akkadian *māru* 'son' is generally connected with Aramaic *måre* 'lord', Arabic *imra'un* 'man', etc. instead of Aramaic *bar*, Arabic *ibnun*, etc., and for the purposes of the present discussion, I have assumed that this is correct. However, in light of the semantic connections between **mr'* and **br'* and between **br'* and **bny*, it is entirely possible that Akkadian *māru* has TWO sets of cognates.

[7] Other instances of Aramaic *r* corresponding to Hebrew *n* are found in Onkelos and Jonathan: *bḥr* = *bḥn* 'to examine' (Gen. 42:15-6, Jer. 9:6, 17:10, 20:12), *ṭmr* = *ṭmn* 'to hide' (Gen. 35:4, Ex. 2:12, Josh. 2:6, 7:21-2, Jer. 13:4-6, etc.), *rṭš* = *nṭš* 'to abandon' (Ex. 23:11, Ju. 6:13, I Sam. 4:2, 17:28, etc.), *ršy* = *nšy* 'to lend' (Ex. 22:24, Deut. 15:2, 24:10-11, II K. 4:1, Jer. 15:10, etc.).

[8] The only evidence I have for a geminated *b* in this word is its Mishnaic Hebrew cognate which appears in Codex Kaufmann as *'arḳubb-* with pronominal suffix and *'arḳov* without.

[9] The earliest attestation of *'uḳbrå* 'muscle' recorded by Payne Smith (1901) is in the Syriac translation of a work by Galen.

EMPHATIC *ḳ* PRECEDED by *r*. Thus, it may well be that the MSA form of this word is due to contamination. However, in view of the fact that the MSA languages are in some respects more archaic than the ancient Semitic languages, it is just possible that they have preserved the original state of affairs more faithfully here as well. In any event, it is worth considering the ramifications of this possibility.

The above-mentioned correspondences are part of a much larger picture shown in Table 1. The following reconstruction is one of a number of possible theories capable of explaining the correspondences given there.

If the word **ʿrḳb* originally meant 'mouse', we may posit the following series of semantic changes in Proto-Semitic:

1) metaphor: 'mouse' (> 'muscle'?) > 'mouse; muscle?; Achilles' tendon, hamstring'

2) metaphor: 'to hamstring' > 'to hamstring; to trick?'

3) metonymy: 'hamstring' > 'hamstring; hock; ham' (all adjacent to each other)

4) metonymy: 'Achilles' tendon' > 'Achilles' tendon; heel' (adjacent to each other)

5) widening: 'Achilles' tendon, hamstring' > 'tendon' > 'any cord or cord-like duct of the body', e.g. 'tendon, nerve, vein, artery'

6) metaphor: 'cord-like duct of the body' > 'cord-like duct of the body; root' (both branch and both convey vital liquids)

We may posit further that, subsequently, three "triliteralized" forms of **ʿrḳb* were created–**ʿḳb* (liquid second radical deleted), **ʿrḳ* (last radical deleted), **ʿḳr* (last two radicals of **ʿrḳ* metathesized)–and that some of the new meanings came to be associated with them. Thus, the meaning 'heel' came to be associated with **ʿḳb*, the meaning 'cord (-like duct) of the body' came to be associated with **ʿrḳ*, and the meaning 'to hamstring' seems to have become associated with **ʿḳr*, while the meanings 'Achilles' tendon; hock; ham' generally remained with **ʿrḳb*. However, the formal differentiation of these meanings was not absolute, which is why we still find variation in Semitic words for 'heel' (Arabic *ʿaqib*, Syriac *ʿeḳbå*, Hebrew *ʿåḳev*, Akkadian *eḳbu*, but Tigre *tərḳub*), 'root' (H *ʾarḳ*, Arabic *ʿirq*, but Syriac *ʿeḳḳårå*, Hebrew *ʿåḳar* 'uproot'), 'tendon, sinew' (Ḥ *ʾarḳ*, Tigre *ʿäräk*, Hebrew *ʿoreḳ*?,[10] Jewish Aramaic and Syriac *ʿeraḳtå* 'strap',[11] but Arabic *ʿaqab*, Ugaritic *ʿḳb*), 'to hamstring' (Arabic *ʿaqara*, Hebrew *ʿiḳḳer*, but also Arabic *ʿarqaba*), and possibly 'to trick, practice deception' (Arabic *ʿarqaba* but Hebrew *ʿåkav*). Indeed, it is this variation (seen in large measure already by Wajnberg (1935:57), which proves that **ʿrḳb*, **ʿḳb*, **ʿrḳ*, and **ʿḳr* are etymologically related.

---

[10] In Job 30:17 the plural of this word occurs in parallelism with *ʿaṣåmim* 'bones'. Its Greek rendering there is νεῦρα 'sinews, nerves'.

[11] It is clear that this Syriac word belongs here, because its semantic relationship with Tigre *ʿäräk* is exactly the same as the semantic relationship between Greek ἱμάς 'strap, thong' and its English cognate *sinew*. Thus, the possibility (considered in Steiner (1977:157)) that the Aramaic words for 'sandal-strap' contain an etymological **ḏ* is to be rejected.

	'mouse jerboa'	(→ 'muscle')	'Achilles' tendon, hamstring' →	'to hamstring'	(→ 'to trick')	'ham, hock'	'heel'	'tendon, sinew' →	'nerve' →	'vein, artery' →	'root' →	'to uproot'
Ḥarsūsi	*'arḳayb*	–	*'arḳayb ḏe fam*	–	–	–	–	*'arḳ*	*'arḳ*	*'arḳ*	*'arḳ*	–
Tigre	*'ekrib* 'badger'	–	–	–	–	*tärḳub*	*tərḳub*	*'äräḳ*	*'äräk*	–	–	–
Arabic	*'akābir* (pl.)	–	*'urqūb*	*'arqaba, 'aqara*	*'arqaba*	*'urqūb*	*'aqib*	*'aqab*	*'irq*	*'irq*	*'irq*	–
Syriac	*'uḳbar(t)å*	*'uḳbartå*	*'arḳubbå*	–	–	*'arḳubbå*	*'eḳbå*	*'eraḳtå* 'strap'	–	–	*'eḳḳårå*	*'ḳar*
Hebrew	*'axbår*	–	–	*'iḳḳer*	*'åḳev*	*'arḳov*	*'åḳev*	*'oreḳ?*	*'oreḳ?*	*'oreḳ?*		*'åḳar*
Old English	*mūs*	*mūs*				*hōh*	*hōh*					
Latin	*musculus*	*musculus*						*nervus*	*nervus*			
Ethiopic		*šərew*						*šərəw*	*šərəw*		*šərəw*	

( ) marks a development which is particularly uncertain
└─┘ connects words with identical roots

Table 1

The above reconstruction is more broadly-based and, I think, more plausible than the older view that the hamstring was conceived of as the "root-sinew" of the body (Brown, Driver and Briggs [1907] s.v. *'ḳr*). It should also be noted that the latter view is incompatible with the notion that the meaning 'hamstring' developed from the meaning 'mouse'.

Before leaving this problem, I would like to call attention to an intriguing possibility, namely, that there might be a connection between **'rḳb* mouse?, hamstring, . . . ' and **'ḳrb* 'scorpion'. It is tempting to see the latter as a metathesized derivative of the former, even if Tigre *'arḳäb* and Mandaic *arḳba*, both meaning 'scorpion', are late innovations. It may be significant that Arabic *'aqrab* 'scorpion' also means 'strap, esp. of a sandal'. The latter is precisely the meaning of Syriac *'eraḳtå (cf.* Onkelos' *'arḳaθ* - and the Genesis Apocryphon's *'rḳ'*), which, as we have already seen,[12] can hardly be separated from Ḥ *'arḳ*, Tigre *'äräḳ*, etc.

This example, together with the ones that preceded it, should be sufficient to show the importance of MSA in general and ḤL in particular. Weighed against that importance, the blemishes of ḤL, to which we now turn, seem almost trivial.

Let me dispose of the misprints first. Only a small number caught my eye: *śäláyt* for *ṣäláyt* (p. xv, l. 19), *šeffέy* for *ṣeffey* (p. 126, l. 9), *ḥägeret* for *ḥägerēt* (p. 57, l. 32, cf. p. 1, l.37 and p. 54, l. 22).

An annoying feature of ḤL which struck me soon after I opened it can be blamed in part on its editors. The "pre-lexical" material of the book is disorganized and repetitious. The pressure of Arabic on Ḥ is discussed both on p. v and on p. x. The inclusion in ḤL of comparative material from other MSA languages is noted both on p. v and on p. xi. The phonology of Arabic loan-words in Ḥ is discussed partly on p. xiii and partly on p. xxvi. This problem may be due in part to the peculiar division of this material into a hybrid "preface-and-acknowledgements" and an "introduction".

Probably the most serious defect of ḤL is its method of analyzing the roots of Ḥ lexical items. The lengthy introduction of the book says virtually nothing about that crucial subject, and I for one am totally baffled. If the roots of ḤL are meant to be synchronic Ḥ roots, why do they contain ', ', and final *w* in cases where the full words contain no traces of these consonants? And if they are meant to be proto-MSA or proto-Semitic roots, why do they contain *h* in cases where other MSA languages (usually Ś) have preserved the original *š*, and even in cases where H itself has preserved it in part, e.g. *mešmē'* 'ear' alongside *hōma* 'to hear'? We may illustrate this problem using the word *ḥérih, ḥerīh* 'head'. Despite the fact that this form (like its MSA cognates) has neither a ' nor a consistently long vowel, ḤL derives it from a medial ' root, reconstructed with the help of comparative Semitics. In dealing with the last radical, however, ḤL ignores both comparative Semitics and internal MSA evidence (Ś *réš*), and winds up with the hybrid root *r'h*.

In addition, there are certain analyses which are difficult to understand and no matter what stage of the language is being described. Why, for instance, should *bāréd* 'gunpowder' be

[12] See the preceding footnote.

considered quinqueliteral and *wāyer* 'wire' be considered quadriliteral, when *'ālem* 'knowledge', *'āmer* 'age, life', *ġāber* (pl. *ġewábber!*) 'she-camel about to bring forth', *ḥālem* 'dream', *ṣāḳer* (pl. *ṣeḳéwwer!*) 'falcon', *ṭāfel* 'baby, child', *yā'ed* (pl. *yewā'ed!*) 'an item of camel gear', and others on this pattern are considered triliteral by ḤL? And why should *meleḥáw* 'side of the jaw' be derived from *mlḥ* rather than *lḥw/y*—the root of its S cognate according to Leslau (1938:244). And finally, what stage of the language is ḤL describing when it gives the root of *arēm* 'to trick a camel into accepting her own young, or a substitute, or a tulchan' as *rm'*? If modern Ḥ, the root should end in *m*. If proto-MSA, the root should be *rm'* (cf. S *ɛrũ'*). If proto-Semitic (assuming that this word goes back that far), the root should be *rmw/y* (cf. Hebrew *rǝmiyyå* 'deceit'). Until Johnstone explains how he arrived at his roots, this otherwise grateful reader of ḤL will be forced to ignore them.

References

BITTNER, Maximilian

1910 "Neues Mehri-Materiale aus dem Nachlasse des Dr. Wilhelm Hein," *Wiener Zeitschrift für die Kunde des Morgenlandes* 24:70-93.

1916 *Studien zur Šḫauri-Sprache in den Bergen von Ḍofâr am Persischen Meerbusen* I. Sitzungsberichte der philosophisch-historischen Klasse der Kaiserl. Akademie der Wissenschaften in Wien 179/2. Vienna: Alfred Hölder.

1917 *Studien . . . Meerbusen* IV. SPHKAWW 183/5. Vienna: Alfred Hölder.

BROWN, Francis, and S. R. Driver and Charles Briggs.

1907 *A Hebrew and English Lexicon of the Old Testament*. Oxford: Clarendon Press.

CARTER, H. J.

1847 "Notes on the Mahrah tribe of Southern Arabia, with a vocabulary of their language, to which are appended additional observations on the Gara tribe." *Journal of the Bombay Branch of the Royal Asiatic Society* 2:339-70.

CATFORD, J. C.

1977 *Fundamental Problems in Phonetics*. Bloomington: Indiana University Press.

CHRISTIAN, V.

1944 *Die Stellung des Mehri innerhalb der semitischen Sprachen*. Sitzungsberichte der philosophisch-historischen Klasse der Kaiserl. Akademie der Wissenschaften in Wien 222/3. Brunn: Rudolf M. Rohrer.

DEGEN, Rainer

1978 "Ḥumšā, ein hebräisches Lehnwort im Syrischen," *Oriens Christianus* 62:53-59.

EILERS, Wilhelm

1971 "Iranisches Lehngut im Arabischen." *Actas do IV Congresso de Estudos Árabes e Islâmicos, Coimbra-Lisboa . . . 1968*, 581-660.

FRESNEL, Fulgence

1838 "Cinquième lettre sur l'histoire des arabes avant l'islamisme" *Journal Asiatique* 6:529-70.

GORDON, Cyrus

1965 *Ugaritic Textbook.* Analecta Orientalia 38. Pontificium Institutum Biblicum.

GREENBERG, Joseph
1970 "Some generalizations concerning glottalic consonants especially implosives," *International Journal of American Linguistics* 36:123-145.

JAHN, Alfred
1902 *Die Mehri-Sprache in Südarabien*. Südarabische Expedition der Kaiserl. Akademie der Wissenschaften in Wien 3. Vienna. Alfred Hölder.

JASTROW, Marcus
1950 *A Dictionary of the Targumim, the Talmud Babli and Yerushalmi, and the Midrashic Literature*. New York: Pardes.

JOHNSTONE, T. M.
1975a "The Modern South Arabian languages," *Afroasiatic Linguistics* 1:93-121.
1975b "Contrasting articulations in the Modern South Arabian languages," In J. and T. Bynon (eds.) *Hamito-Semitica*, pp. 155-9. The Hague: Mouton.

LESLAU, Wolf
1938 *Lexique soqoṭri*. Collection Linguistique publiée par la Société de Linguistique de Paris. Paris: C. Klincksieck.
1958 *Ethiopic and South Arabic Contributions to the Hebrew Lexicon*. University of California Publications in Semitic Philology 20. Berkeley, Los Angeles: University of California Press.

MAS'ŪDĪ, al-.
1861 *Les prairies d'or* (C. Barbier de Meynard and Pavet de Courteille, eds.), I. Paris: Imprimerie Imperiale.
1865 *Les prairies d'or* (C. Barbier de Meynard, ed.), IV. Paris: Imprimerie Imperiale.

PARDEE, Dennis
1978 "A Philological and Prosodic Analysis of the Ugaritic Serpent Incantation *UT* 607," *The Journal of the Ancient Near Eastern Society of Columbia University* 10:73-108.

PAYNE SMITH, Robert
1901 *Thesaurus Syriacus*. Oxford: Clarendon Press.

ROSITZKE, Harry
1939 "A further note on Welsh *ll* and Icelandic *hl*." *Le Maître Phonétique* 65:7-8.

SCHUH, Russell G.
1979 Review of *The Case for Fricative-Laterals in Proto-Semitic* by Richard Steiner. *Language* 55:256.

STEINER, Richard
1977 *The Case for Fricative-Laterals in Proto-Semitic*. American Oriental Series 59. New Haven: American Oriental Society.

THOMAS, Bertram
1937 "Four strange tongues from South Arabia," *Proceedings of the British Academy* 23:231-331.

VON SODEN, Wolfram
1959- *Akkadisches Handwörterbuch*. Wiesbaden: Harrassowitz.

WAJNBERG, I.
1935 "Etude sur les quadrilitères tigriña." *Rocznik Orientalistyczny* 11:52-78.

YUSHMANOV, N. V.
1930 "Dannye Fresnel'ya o južno-arabskom narečii eẋkili." *Akademiia nauk SSSR, Aziatskii muzei, Zapiski kollegii, Vostokovedov . . . Moscow* 5:379-91.

Günther Schlee, ***Sprachliche Studien zum Rendille*** (Hamburger Philologische Studien, 46). Hamburg: Helmut Buske, 1978. vii, 166 pp., 1 map.
By HANS-JÜRGEN SASSE (University of Munich)

The study of Cushitic languages has always profited form the work of outsiders. Anthropologists, missionaries and historians have probably contributed more to our knowledge in this field than the professional Cushiticists themselves (if there have ever existed any). The present book is the work of such an outsider, Günther Schlee, who learned to speak an East Cushitic language (Rendille, North Kenya) during ethnological field work among the Rendille and, after his return, decided to publish his linguistic notes as a supplement to his ethnological work (Schlee 1978). It is a slim volume which consists of three parts: a grammatical sketch, sample texts, and a glossary. The grammatical part (p. 1-31, with an English summary, p. 31-49) is disappointingly tiny, but in view of the paucity of published Rendille data, any new information is welcome. The same must be said of the glossary (p. 107-166) that boastfully numbers 1132 items, most of which, however, turn out to be different grammatical forms of the same lexical entries; discarding these, the lexical information actually given is reduced to approximately 50%. By far the most interesting section is the collection of texts that forms the central part of the book (p. 50-106); it is of particular importance both because there is no better way of getting acquainted with the structure of a language than by texts (and there is unfortunately a general dearth of Cushitic texts), and because thanks to the author's profound ethnological knowledge, the collection goes beyond a mere presentation to include a penetration of their content.

Schlee's book could be taken to represent an important contribution to the study of Rendille, were it not for the fact that the way it is executed leaves much to be desired. Initiative to learn the language of the people studied is by no means a necessary prerequisite among ethnologists (especially in Germany), so the author's effort as such must be praised. He appears to have had considerable linguistic training (he must have taken quite a number of courses in the theory of grammar and in contemporary methods of linguistic analysis); there are, however, certain points in his analysis that raise doubts as to whether he is actually able to apply what he has learned. It is this lack of linguistic "feeling" that reduces the value of Schlee's work to a minimum. First of all, his diction is that of a touristic language guide: primitive, diffuse and unprecise. He needs a whole page to tell the reader that the Rendille verb consists of stem and affixes, and another whole page to acquaint him with the fact that deletions of adjacent vowels at word boundaries, which occur in casual speech, may destroy the regular appearance of grammatical forms and are therefore not represented in the phonemic transcription (p. 3-4). On the other hand, important topics like the function of the verbal focus prefix *á-* (on which cf. below) or the function of the pitch accent and its role in morphology and syntax are hardly touched on. On *á-*, for instance, all we are told is that the prefix "has no meaning" (p. 107), and that it is "very often encountered" (p. 3). The treatment of the pitch accent is confined to the mere mention of its existence.

Schlee's inability to express himself in a linguistically adequate manner often leads to a certain clumsiness in his statements, e.g. "den Dependent finden wir z.B. in relativer Bedeutung", apparently intended to mean that the "Dependent", i.e. subjunctive, paradigm occurs in relative clauses, and to a number of redundancies (his *ü* and *ö* are allophones of *u* and *o*, as he himself admits right from the start; it is therefore unnecessary to have extra symbols for them, wrong to call them phonemes and to enclose them in diagonals, and even worse to call them umlaut). This inability also tends to give rise to false statements like this: "Durch die Unterscheidung solcher Formen kommen wir zu fünf verschiedenen Aspekten . . . Imperfekt . . . Perfekt . . . Dependent . . . Negativ-Imperfekt . . . Negativ-Perfekt" (p. 4). There are universally only two aspects, namely perfective and imperfective. The negative counterparts of their positive paradigms are not themselves aspects, just as in English the negative present is certainly the same tense as the positive present. The "Dependent" (I prefer to call it "subjunctive"; it is the common East Cushitic paradigm in *-o*) is of course not an aspect at all; it is a verbal paradigm with primarily modal and secondarily subordinative functions.

Linguistic naïveté is not, however, responsible for all of the shortcomings of this book. There is also a good deal of misinterpretation and, last but not least, sloppiness. Misinterpretation, or perhaps misperception, is responsible for a number of oddities in the transcription. I do not have Schlee's experience in Rendille,[1] but I am sure that no Rendille pronounces *ani* 'I', *ati* 'thou', *atin* 'ye' with a geminate (*anni, atti, attin*), as Schlee would have it. At least none of my informants did so, and it would also be historically unjustified, as well. I suspect that German orthography played a certain role in the choice of this transcription. The same is true of forms such as *dellen* 'they gave birth' (stem *del-*), *nassa* 'I rest' (1s imperfect of *nas-*) and similar forms with both historically and morphophonemically unjustified geminates. Other transcriptions that I do not trust include: *ibe̱e̱n* 'night' (should be *ibēn*), *ilakh* 'tooth' (probably *ilah*), *dökh* 'hole' (should be *doh*), *don-* 'love' (probably *dōn-*). Sloppiness is particularly apparent in the glossary. The author often fails to indent material that belongs to the same lemma and, conversely, indents lemmata that do not belong under their heading, which makes the glossary extremely difficult to use. Moreover, a number of forms with proclitic elements are listed under the initial letters of the proclitic elements, e.g. *á-yumui* 'he died' is written *áyumui* and is listed as an extra form under *a*.

I would have been far more generous in my examination of Schlee's linguistic style, were it not for the fact that he himself criticized a linguist's description of Rendille in a fairly arrogant way. This criticism is found in a rather strange place, namely in the English summary of the grammar which occupies a special position in the book. It is a summary in name only; in reality it is a critical examination of Heine's (1975/76) Rendille article,[2] which reads almost like a personal attack and was apparently written exclusively for this reason: harsh words, lack of tolerance and a strange mania to prove Heine wrong wherever possible are its outstanding characteristics. Paradoxically enough, there seems to be no obvious reason for such a behavior. Heine's article is admittedly full of mistakes, but one should not forget that it was a pioneer work (the first presentation of a relatively large quantity of Rendille material ever) and part of an extensive survey covering ALL Kenyan languages. Be that as it may, I would like to make use of the opportunity of this review to discuss some of the "open [*sic*] problems of Rendille grammar" (this is the title of Schlee's "summary') that were subject of the controversy from my own, I hope more objective, viewpoint.

[1] I worked with informants in Nairobi and Marsabit for only a few days.
[2] Schlee cites it incorrectly as "Notes on Rendille Language" on p. 31.

First of all, there is the problem of vowel representation. According to Schlee, Rendille has ten vowel phonemes, whereas Heine distinguishes only five. Although my own notes likewise indicate only five vowels (perhaps because I expected to find five vowels and did not have enough time to convince myself of the contrary), I am inclined to believe Schlee on this point, especially in view of the fact that the closely related languages Somali and Boni also have a ten vowel system (with two categories, tense and lax, and a tendency towards vowel harmony). I concede, however, that the question of vowel tenseness in the Omo-Tana languages (of which Somali, Boni, and Rendille are members) is a particularly vexed one, so the solution of the problem should be left to future research.

As for consonants, I am sure that a distinction between /d̪/ and /d/ is significant, although Schlee denies it. The difference is admittedly hard to perceive for the phonetically inexperienced observer, but it is supported by etymological correspondences. Unfortunately, most of Heine's examples of the contrast are wrong. As for Heine's opposition between a glottal /h/ and a pharyngeal /ħ/, Schlee is probably right in stating that there is only one *h*-phoneme with an allophonically varying degree of pharyngeality. On the other hand, I seem to have a number of minimal pairs. One of these, /huṅ-/ 'pierce' vs. /ħun-/ 'eat', is confirmed by Schlee himself, who distinguishes *hunn-* from *hünn-* (both with a phonemically incorrect geminate, cf. above). Since Schlee's *ü* is an unfailing indicator of pharyngeality, whereas his *u* occurs in pharyngeal as well as in non-pharyngeal contexts, there are two possible explanations: either the two words are homonymous, in which case both Schlee and I failed to perceive pharyngeality in the word for 'pierce' (and, by implication, our joint misperception in the same word is entirely fortuitous), or there is really a difference in pharyngeality between these words, in which case the theory of the two *h*-phonemes becomes highly probable. In other words, this problem also awaits future research.

When Schlee attempts morphology (p. 38), he hardly has better footing than Heine. There is a mysterious "suffix -e" which has been the subject of much controversy (cf. also Oomen [1977] and Hudson [1977]). Heine distinguished two *-e*'s, one with a neutral tone which was said to represent the accusative case marker of feminine nouns, and one with a high tone which was said to be a locative suffix. Both descriptions are wrong; however, Heine was partly right in attributing a case function to one of these suffixes, only he failed to pin-point the right one. Schlee, on the other hand, states that the *-e* suffix "has expressive and ordinative functions and can by no means be considered a case ending". He further believes that it "can always be omitted without causing any changes to the basic meaning of the sentence". Both Heine and Schlee failed to recognize that there are at least three *e*'s with entirely different functions. The first is a subject case ending of a certain inflectional class of Rendille nouns (corresponding historically to the suffix *-i* of the fourth declension of Somali nouns). This *-e* is part of the word and cannot be omitted without semantic change, just as, say, the *-s* of the English word *gives* cannot be omitted without its ceasing to be 3rd person singular present. The second *-e*, which is suffixed to verb forms, occurs at the end of subordinate clauses and has a subordinative (purposive, consecutive, etc.) function which was briefly described by Hudson (1977). The third *-e* (with a high tone) is part of the focus structure of the Rendille sentence. This structure has been very carefully described by Oomen (1977, 1978). It can be reduced to the following, quite simplified statement: There is a basic distinction between noun focus and verb focus. The latter is indicated by the particle *á* which is prefixed (or, better, procliticized) to the verb complex. This is the mysterious particle *á* referred to above, which was taken by Schlee to have "no meaning". If the sentence contains a focalized non-verbal constituent, *á* is omitted. Non-verbal focus constructions must be further subdivided into two classes: non-emphatic and emphatic. In the non-emphatic construction the focalized constituent is put in front of the verb complex where it in a sense replaces the *á*. An emphasized non-verbal focus constituent is followed by *é*; it may appear at any place in the clause except after the verb. Example:

> *lúm á-gelise* 'she PUT (them into) a cave' (Verb-Focus)
> *lúm gelise* 'she put (them into) A CAVE' (Non Verbal-Focus: non-emph.)
> *lúm é gelise* 'it was a cave where she put them' (Non-Verbal-Focus: emphatic)

I would not like to end without mentioning a number of positive aspects, since the book under review should not be regarded as altogether valueless. First of all, it has to be pointed out once again that the most valuable portion of the book is the sample text collection. It would be extremely helpful for the study of East Cushitic if Schlee could be persuaded to publish his entire text collection in the form of a monograph. Secondly, the English summary contains what can be called the first serious attempt to tackle the problem of verbal aspect (imperfective vs. perfective) in an East Cushitic Language (p. 41-45). Schlee gives ample evidence that the verbal paradigms of Rendille do not signalize tense distinctions but rather represent grammatical categories comparable to the category of aspect in the Slavic languages, i.e. they do not indicate time levels, but rather whether the action is conceived by the speaker as punctual/completed or as ongoing. This has often been claimed, sometimes denied, e.g. by Zaborski, but never proved. Another interesting piece of information is the agreement rules (p. 25-28. 48-49), and in particular the apparent conflict between grammatically sanctioned and natural, i.e. number- and sex-oriented, agreement.

To sum up, as Cushiticists, we are grateful to the author for providing us with his contribution to our field. But in view of his rare practical knowledge of the language, he could have done more. If he had organized his findings in the format of a traditional grammatical description without too much theoretical eclecticism, if he had desisted just a little more from prejudice and polemics, he could have given us a fine preliminary documentation of this interesting and important language.

References

HEINE, B.
1975/76 "Notes on the Rendille language (Kenya)." *Afrika und Übersee* 59:175-223.

HUDSON, R.
1977 "Rendille syntax." Unpublished paper.

OOMEN, A.
1977 "Aspects of the Rendille language–Focus in the Rendille Clause." M. A. Diss., University of Nairobi.
1978 "Focus in the Rendille clause." *Studies in African Linguistics* 9:35-65.

SCHLEE, G.
1978 *Das Glaubens- und Sozialsystem der Rendille, Kamelnomaden Nordkenias.* Marburger Studien zur Afrikan- und Asienkunde, 16. Berlin: Dietrich Reimer.

ZABORSKI, A.
1975 *Studies in Hamito-Semitic I: The Verb in Cushitic*. Krakow: Naktadem Uniwersytetu Jagiellońskiego.

Russell G. Schuh, *Bole-Tangale Languages of the Bauchi Area (Northern Nigeria)* (Marburger Studien Zur Afrika und Asienkunde, Serie A, Band 13) Berlin, Dietrich Reimer, 1978, pp. xii, 159, DM 28.

By A. NEIL SKINNER, (University of Wisconsin)

In this work, Schuh has again made a useful contribution to Chadic (and Afroasiatic) studies, by recording for others the results of a three and a half day field trip in Bauchi State in 1975. The languages dealt with are Bele, Kirfi, Galambu, Gera and Geruma, members of the same southern subgroup of Bole-Tangale as Tangale, Pero and Kanakuru. These latter three have received some attention from scholars, in particular Newman (1974), but those recorded by Schuh had previously been available only in minimal lists by Gowers. (Apparently lists recorded by Kraft and referred to in Kraft (1971) were never published [but see now notice on Kraft (1981), this volume—eds.]). So this work in some measure fills in a gap in our knowledge of Chadic, though of course the author does not suggest that the last word has been said on any of the languages recorded during such a brief visit.

For each language an outline of the nominal and verbal systems and a vocabulary, Chadic-English, are given. At the end of the book there is an English and Hausa list of some 400 entries, with glosses in some or all of the languages concerned, e.g.

water (ruwa) Be *àmmá*, Ki *àmmá*, Ga *àmá*, Ge *hàmá*, Gm *àmmá*
lie down (kwanta) Ki *shán-kò*, Ga *sán-àalá*, Ge *sîn-mí*, Gm *sànaá* (KS)
(KS refers to an unpublished list by Shimizu).

Such a list is a welcome addition to comparative studies, though more cross-referencing would help. "Heart" and "liver" need simultaneous scrutiny, as Shimizu found. Also, in the eliciting, it can be helpful to offer more than one Hausa form, e.g. *gora* as well as *sanda* for stick; perhaps *rik̂a* as well as *kama* for 'hold, catch'. This may prove stimulating to informants. But the list as a whole seems to be one based on sound experience. Apart from this, however, Schuh has wisely limited his comments and thoughts on matters comparative to his Introduction. There he is able to use, in addition to the data recorded in this work, his much more extensive studies in the northern subgroup of Bole-Tangale, particularly into verb morphology.

The languages of the Bauchi area, other than Hausa, are unlikely to go on to being spoken for very much longer. Some, in fact, have recently become extinct. This makes Schuh's work the more valuable. When we add the contributions made by Shimizu (1978), Margaret Skinner (1979), and the present writer (1977), we find that what was an empty quarter of Chadic studies has become in a few years very much less so. Comparativists owe a debt to Jungraithmayr at Marburg and Newman at Leiden (formerly at Kano) for their encouragement and assistance in making this possible. It is now, in fact, likely that some of the non-Chadic languages of the area are more in need of recording before they pass into extinction.

Bibliography

KRAFT, Charles H.

1971 "A note on lateral fricatives in Chadic." *Studies in African Linguistics* 2:271-281.

NEWMAN, Paul

1974 *The Kanakuru Language*. West African Language Monographs, 9. Leeds: Institute of Modern English Language Studies in Association with The West African Linguistic Society.

SHIMIZU, Kiyoshi

1978 "The Southern Bauchi Group of Chadic Languages." *Africana Marburgensia*, Sonderheft 2.

SKINNER, Margaret G.

1979 "Aspects of Pa'anci Grammar." Doctoral dissertation, University of Wisconsin [University Microfilms 79-22836, Ann Arbor, Michigan].

SKINNER, A. Neil

1977 "North Bauchi Chadic Languages: Common Roots." *Afroasiatic Linguistics*, 4/1:1-49.

SUGIA – Sprache und Geschichte in Afrika, Band 1 – 1979, edited by: I. Fodor, B. Heine, W. J. G. Möhlig, F. Rottland, R. Vossen, J. Chr. Winter, published by Helmut Buske Verlag, Hamburg, pp. 227.
By ANDRZEJ ZABORSKI, Cracow

The name *SUGIA* may sound African but it is only an abbreviation of the German title *Sprache und Geschichte in Afrika* (Language and History in Africa) of the new scholarly periodical published by the very active Institute of African Studies of the University of Cologne. One volume is to be published per year but on the same page (back of the title) we read that it "Zerscheint in loser Folge".[1] There is no introductory editorial in this opening volume but in the Information for Contributors (p. 226) we read that "all contributions should have a historical perspective which may be confined to one discipline only, e.g. general history, archaeology, linguistics. Preference will be given to articles aiming at an integration of historical linguistics and other historical disciplines." Thus emphasis is put on the cooperation of historical linguistics (in a very broad sense, I believe) and history or rather prehistory of African peoples. This is an interesting combination and we hope that the editors find enough contributors writing on the prehistory and history of both peoples and their languages. In the first volume only one author, Roland Oliver, is a historian, the rest (nine in number) are linguists.

Perhaps it would be better to group articles according to their subjects. So far they are rather dispersed. There are two articles discussing the prehistory of Bantu: R. Oliver looks for Bantu cradle land in Cameroun (pp. 7-20) and W. J. G. Möhlig writes on "The Bantu nucleus: its conditional nature and its prehistorical significance", (pp. 109-142). I think that Oliver might have revised some of his statements if he had seen Möhlig's paper. Apart from Oliver's article there is only one article on history written by J. Chr. Winter (a linguist!) who concentrates

[1] Volume 2 has already appeared in 1980.

on the languages of the whole of the African continent and its prehistoric implications. This article could have been put at the very beginning of the volume. Three articles discuss particular cases of language contact: one by Inge Hofmann, "Sprachkontakte in Nubien zur meroitischen Zeit" (pp. 21-36), deals with the interference between Meroitic and an Afroasiatic language (Beja?) in antiquity; another by Bernd Heine, Franz Rottland, Rainer Vossen, "Proto-Baz: some aspects of early Nilotic-Cushitic contacts" (pp. 75-92), deals with loan words from an extinct Cushitic language in Nilotic; finally Hans-Jürgen Sasse, "Entlehnung morphophonemischer Regeln im Boni" (pp. 93-108), deals with the influence of Oromo morphonemics on another Cushitic language (Boni). Finally there are two articles discussing theoretical problems of contact and especially of pidginization and creolization: Gabriel Manessy writes on "Pidginisation, créolisation, évolution des langues" (pp. 55-74), and Ekkehard Wolff discusses "Sprachkontakt and Ethnizität" (pp. 143-174).

Here are some remarks on articles dealing with Afroasiatic languages. In his article Heine presents various problems connected with the classification of the languages of Africa proposed by Joseph Greenberg which, as it is known, after much debate has been accepted finally (though with reservations concerning details) after more than a quarter of a century. Heine accepts the existence of Khoisan family but says that "further research is required on the position of the East African Khoisan languages Sandawe and Hadza" (p. 38). It should be mentioned here that in the paper entitled "The classification of Hadza" presented at a seminar in the Department of Foreign Languages and Linguistics of the University of Dar es Salaam, E. D. Elderkin indicates a number of common lexical items and even some grammatical parallels between Hadza and Omotic suggesting that there is still a possibility of an Afroasiatic affiliation of Hadza. In a private letter dated 30 April 1981 Elderkin writes me, "I'm currently still working on Sandawe, which to a classifier could only be Khoisan." Heine uses the name "Erythraic" instead of "Afroasiatic" following Reinisch, Tucker, and Bryan. Actually it is not entirely correct to say that the hypothesis about Omotic (formerly West Cushitic) being a separate branch of Afroasiatic that has been elaborated by both Fleming and Bender and, as a matter of fact, going back to Herma Plazikowsky-Brauner, is justified by both lexical and grammatical evidence (p. 42). In his book, *Omotic: a New Afroasiatic Language Family* (University Museum Studies, Southern Illinois University, Carbondale, 1975), Bender says (p. 224) that on the basis of grammar, Omotic can be classified as an independent branch of Afroasiatic but on the evidence of lexicon it can be classified as going back to a common ancestor with Cushitic. In my opinion which I expressed in a note addressed to the 1980 Conference on Ethiopian Studies in Jerusalem entitled "Can Omotic be reclassified as West Cushitic?" I emphasize that we still know too little about Omotic languages and the possibility that they really belong to Cushitic has not been eliminated especially since it is possible that we have concentrated so far only on some innovating, i.e. not conservative or archaic, languages of this group. It is possible that Janjero, for example, is conservative or archaic enough that it shows some grammatical affiliation to Cushitic that cannot be explained by interference in spite of the fact that interference has worked indeed in various realms. As far as common vocabulary is concerned Heine (note 17, p. 49) quotes Fleming's calculation of the common basic vocabulary around 12% in the case of Cushitic and Omotic while in note 16 Fleming is again quoted saying that the rates of cognates shared by various branches of Afroasiatic lie between 4 and 10%. Thus, Cushitic-Omotic percentages are very high (cf. Bender!). As far as Chadic is concerned I think that we should finally stop mentioning that "some linguists like Marcel Cohen would prefer to exclude Chadic from

Erythraic" even in a footnote (n.13, p. 49). If "some linguists" that have some doubts in this respect really exist after more than a quarter of a century, this is due only to unnecessary mechanical repetition of this outdated opinion. Heine says that "Proto-Erythraic" is likely to go back at least to the 4th or 5th millennium B.C." (p. 42). This is only a matter of intuition. Personally I think that Proto-Afroasiatic period goes back several millennia more since already about 3000 B.C. Egyptian and Akkadian were already so different. Obviously it is extremely difficult to estimate the rate or "speed" of language change and diversification—this may be rather fast or very slow depending on circumstances. On the original homeland of Afroasiatic Heine says that Ethiopian Highlands region is one possible area (p. 42). As we know, Sahara has been another hypothetical cradleland and a later hypothesis by Diakonoff has indicated the Sudanese part of the Nile Valley. Closing these remarks I have to emphasize that Heine provides a very useful synthesis of the existing genetic classification of African languages with many important conclusions.

The article by H.-J. Sasse on the borrowing of morphonemic rules in Boni (a Cushitic language spoken in Kenya, closely related to Somali and Rendille) is a good contribution mainly because it brings new data on the little known southern Orma dialect of Oromo (formerly known as Galla) and on Boni with a number of remarks on dialect differences and interference phenomena. Although on p. 105 Sasse strongly emphasises that "borrowing" of some morphonemic rules by Boni from Orma has been possible because the conjugational morphemes and conjugational patterns in which these rules operate are extremely similar, nevertheless in other parts of the articles he is rather inclined to suggest that borrowing of morphonemic rules may occur without such an immense morphological relationship (almost identity!) of two not distinctly related languages. In particular a reader who can read only the English and French summaries is left without this crucial remark and may gain a wrong impression that the author advocates borrowing of morphonemic rules without borrowing morphemes. Actually Sasse attacks the traditional idea that morphonemic structure usually is highly indicative of genetic relationship and on the evidence of Boni claims that this is not necessarily true. This is weakened by the fact that in Boni we find a lot of phonological, morphological, and lexical evidence that indicates the direct relationship with Somali, more distant with Orma and Oromo in general, so that it is not really necessary, in this particular case, to classify by taking morphonemics into consideration at all. This case of Boni-Orma morphonemic interference is not very surprising since both related morphological systems of these languages have been very similar when they came into contact so that actually there was no question of morphological "borrowing" and what could be "borrowed", i.e. transferred, were just morphonemic rules that have been different. In short, I do not think that this Boni-Orma inteference brings much support for a revision of the existing theory of interference and language change. The article, as a whole, is important as a solid study of a particular case based on new data.

The article entitled "Proto-Baz: some aspects of early Nilotic-Cushitic contacts" by B. Heine, F. Rottland and R. Vossen is an attempt at reconstructing the phonemic inventory of an extinct Cushitic language on the basis of the Cushitic lexical borrowings in the Nilotic languages. They propose to call this unknown extinct language "Proto-Baz", the name being derived from the East Cushitic root "baz" meaning "lake", probably Lake Turkana. This is an important contribution to the problem of Cushitic-Nilotic contacts following C. Ehret's books on the problem. It is particularly noteworthy that it is a joint result of specialists on both Nilotic and Cushitic. While the hypothesis about an extinct Cushitic language (why not a group of closely related languages?) is probable, nevertheless I should hesitate to suggest, as the authors do (p. 80), to classify this "Proto-Baz" as an independent group of Omo-Tana branch of Lowland East Cushitic parallel to Proto-Sam (now represented by Somali, Boni, and Rendille), Baiso, and still enigmatic "Galaboid" which tentatively groups Dasenech, Elmolo, and still rather unknown Arbore. I do not think that sound correspondences established on the basis of some forty loan-words really allow such a classification. In any case this very hypothetical character of "Proto-Baz" classification should be indicated somehow, e.g. with an asterisk or question mark, in the auxiliary "genealogical tree" on p. 80. It is noteworthy that most of the loan-words have cognates in Sam languages and there is only one case when a cognate is found only in Dasenech, Arbore, and Bayso but not in "Sam", and there is also only one cognate exclusively with Elmolo. As far as the map of Cushitic-Nilotic contacts is concerned (p. 84), I do not understand why it is claimed that it represents a situation between 1000 B.C. and just 100 A.D. This "100 A.D." looks like an attempt to extend the time-span into "common era" but does an idea of such an era make sense in this East African context? In general, as far as dating is concerned, many linguists follow a practice of a rather intuitive dating as a substitute for the rejected glottochronological calculation. Of course even an intuitive dating is better than nothing, but sometimes, when historians or anthropologists establish dating on the basis of another hypothetical dating of linguists, there is a danger of compounding of errors. In this very volume R. Oliver takes for granted that around the second millennium B.C. "Bantu was evolving as a single language" (p. 16). This is extremely tentative though at the same time he uses and combines with it highly precise radiocarbon dating!

Another article on Afroasiatic deals with Southern Cushitic Aasax. It is by Jürgen Christoph Winter who is practically the only man who has been able to collect some significant data on this language which is most probably extinct now. Practically this is a study of the history of Aasax people since the end of the 19th century with a focus on their relation to the Maasai which led to the total "Maasaization" of Aasax. A very long footnote (no. 2, almost five pages!) practically contains a history of the study of Aasax language if we can speak about the history of the study of a language which still remains almost unknown. There is no doubt that this contribution provides an important historical and sociolinguistic background for any research of Aasax language, but facts about this language, i.e. the publication of the data on this language, are badly needed. We may hope that Winter's presumably rich collection of Aasax language material will soon appear.

With a solid philological apparatus Inge Hofmann provides facts about historical contacts between the speakers of Meroitic, Nubian, and possibly Afroasiatic languages. He suggests that prefixes *te* /feminine/ and *ye-* /masculine/ that occur with names in Meroitic inscriptions (if the philological analysis of Meroitic is correct in this case!) may be a borrowing from an Afroasiatic language, e.g. from Beja. The problem is, however, why just prefixes like that should be "borrowed"? We should expect at first lexical and syntactic interference as a prerequisite for a morphological interference.

In the first theoretical article Manessy says that "pidginization and creolization are not to be considered as exceptional phenomena which are connected with particular situation of contacts; they are continuous processes resulting respectively from a weakening and the reinforcement of the socio-cultural standards" (p. 74). Thus pidginization and creolization should, according to the author, occur in the evolution of every language. In my opinion we may call every "simplification" of language structure a "pidginization" and every change toward "regularity", "symmetry", etc. may be eventually called "creolization" but what for? In my view such a considerable widening of the meaning of the terms "pidginization" and "creolization" is unnecessary and actually misleading. Pidginization occurs only when speakers who create a pidgin have only an incomplete and imperfect knowledge of the language which they "pidginize", i.e. there is no true or full bilingualism in such a case and only parts of two languages interfere, in many cases quite at random. This is one of the obvious differences between pidginization *sensu stricto* and other types of language contact and interference including interdialectal contact and interference.

The second article on theory of language contact by Wolff is an attempt at constructing an abstract theory of language contact. It would have been better to provide more concrete examples of the particular cases. Personally I do not believe in the use of the concept of "mixed languages". The article is rich in interesting though abstract thoughts.

In general the new periodical collects papers of high standards and its original profile that differs it from all other periodicals is an editorial success.

II. SHORT NOTICES

C. Ébobissé, ***Die Morphologie des Verbs im Ost-Dangaleat*** (Guera, Tschad). Marburger Studien zur Afrika- und Asienkunde. Serie A: Afrika, Band 21, Berlin: Dietrich Reimer, 1979, pp. 158

Dangaleat, an East Chadic language spoken in central Chad Republic, is becoming one of the best documented of all Chadic languages. Several publications of J. Fédry, especially his *Dictionnaire dangaléat* (Lyon: Afrique et Langage, 1971), which is surpassed in size among Chadic language dictionaries only by the great Hausa dictionaries, present data from the western dialect. E's book is on the eastern dialect,* but by all indications, the two dialects differ mainly in tones only. This is the first large grammatical work on Dangaleat. Its scope is broader than the title indicates. E's method was to work from a sizeable corpus of texts plus an 800 sentence questionnaire in order to analyze the verbal system. The book therefore considers verbs in their syntactic contexts and presents many example sentences illustrating verb use.

Following an introduction presenting background on the language and field work and a short chapter on phonology, the chapters on the verbal system per se are as follows: 2. Morphologie der verbalen Grundform, 3. Das Verb im selbständigen Satz, 5. Zusammengesetzte Formen: Direktional, 6. Das Verb im unselbständigen Satz: Relativformen, 7. Negation, and 8. Defektives Verb: zà "sagen". Chapter 9 is a summary of the main objectives of the book, and this

* There is also a large dictionary of this dialect by P. de Montgolfier (*Vocabulaire dangalèat. Kaawo daŋla*, Lyon, 1973), but this seems to be virtually unobtainable, at least outside Chad.

is followed by an Appendix listing the 900 + verbs studied, organized according to morphological class.

E's presentation follows a straightforward descriptive model with plenty of nicely arranged data. The book will be valuable for Chadicists, Afroasiaticists, and linguists who might wish to apply formal theories to the areas where Dangaleat is richest, viz. marking verbal distinctions through phonologically and morphologically conditioned vowel and tone alternations ("Apophonie" and "Apotonie"). [R.G.S.]

Lionel Galand, ***Langue et littérature bèrberes.*** Vingt cinq ans d'études. (Chroniques de l'Etudes sur les Sociétés Méditerranéennes). Centre des Recherches Centre National de la Recherche Scientifique, 1979, 205 pp.

This book reproduces in one volume eleven annotated bibliographic surveys of Berber studies that appeared in the *Annuaire de l'Afrique du Nord* (vols. 4-14) covering the years 1954-1975, with an additional, as yet unpublished survey for 1976-1977. Each chapter is introduced by news of Berberologists, of meetings, of the teaching of Berber, and by an account of surveys, bibliographies. The first major division surveys studies on the origin, history and genetic relationships of Berber, classified according to the directions of the comparison. This is followed by a geographically classified account of linguistic studies on Berber dialects, first the general ones then the dialect-specific ones. Finally, a section deals with Berber literature. Each item mentioned carries a serial number. Altogether 1512 publications are treated, an impressive number showing how vigorous the field is. For technical reasons, the twelve "chronicles" were not telescoped together so as to provide continuous 25-year accounts of each topic. Yet the present format, complete with a general subject index and an author index, is very clear and easy to use. One should be very grateful to Professor Galand for producing such a useful tool for the study of Berber. One wishes there were comparable surveys in the other domains of Afroasiatic. [R.H.]

H. Jungraithmayr (ed.), ***Struktur und Wandel afrikanischer Sprachen*** (Vorträge vom XX. Deutschen Orientalistentag, Erlangen 1977). Marburger Studien zur Afrika- und Asienkunde, Serie A: Afrika, Band 17, Berlin: Dietrich Reimer, 1978, pp. iv, 189. DM32.

As the subtitle indicates, this volume is a collection of papers presented in 1977 at the Deutsche Orientalistentage, a series of meetings held every three to four years. The subjects of the papers and the languages discussed are diverse, since, as J states in his preface, there was no attempt to follow a unified theme. Almost half the volume is devoted to a survey paper by Robert G. Armstrong, "The development of Fulani Studies: a linguist's view". While no serious linguist believes that Fulani is an Afroasiatic language, the damage done in Meinhof's *Sprachen der Hamiten* persists even today in reference works and library card catalogues, which call the Fulani and their language "Hamitic". Armstrong critiques previous literature on Fulani and presents an incontrovertible demonstration of its Niger-Congo affiliation, if such a demonstration were needed.

Of the remaining seven papers, there is one on Meroitic (I. Hofmann, "Die Gottheiten in der Invokationsformel der meroitischen Totentexte"), three on Niger-Congo (L. Gerhardt, "Benue-Kongo oder Benue-Kwa?"; W. J. G. Möhlig, "Synchrone Faktoren des Sprachwandels im Savannen-Bantu"; T. C. Schadeberg, "Partizipanten am Dialog: Eine grammatische Kategorie, nachgewiesen am Bantu"), and three on Afroasiatic languages. This note will consider only the latter three.

H. Jungraithmayr's contribution, "Gebrochene Plurale im Mubi (Ost-Tschad)", describes the pervasive pluralization of *both* nouns and verbs in Mubi (an East Chadic language spoken in Chad Republic) through internal vowel alternation and/or consonant gemination. He questions a hypothesis of Z. Frajzyngier's that Chadic nominal plurals arose from verbal plurals by noting the improbability that broken nominal plurals could have arisen this way independently in East and West Chadic as well as Semitic, Berber, and Cushitic. An appendix illustrates all the classes of Mubi broken nominal plurals.

G. Schlee, in "Soziale, Kosmologische und mythologische Bezüge der Verben 'herauskommen' und 'sich drehen' im Rendille", shows how the living environment and the social and cosmological systems of the Rendille explain the apparently "unusual" way (from a German translation point of view) certain words are used. Thus, a verb roughly translatable as "herauskommen" refers to men who have undergone certain rights of passage as well as the germination of plants. A verb roughly translatable as "sich drehen" is applied to events seen as part of a cosmological cycle.

E. Wolff's contribution, "Strukturelle Merkmale oral tradierter Ein-Satz-Literatur der Lamang", is in a sense complementary to Schlee's. Whereas Schlee presents an ethnographic study, showing how social organization is reflected in a restricted area of speech, Wolff presents a structural linguistic study showing organizational patterns in a restricted type of oral literature, which, of course, is inextricably embedded in culture. He concentrates on that variety of *Ein-Satz-Literatur* called Gwad Hwara ("proverbs") taken in a very broad sense).* He keeps his "semantic remarks", the normal staple of literary analysis, to a minimum, concentrating on a linguistic structure. In his structural analysis, he considers stylistic transformations from "basic" syntax and consonantal, vocalic, and tonal rimes. While he presents convincing cases of rimes and structural parallelisms from phrase to phrase in his examples, the skeptical linguist might question to what extent these are chance features in the examples chosen. Still, the explicitness of his method has the advantage of testability over a larger body of data as well as the possibility of application to similar genres across languages. [R.G.S.]

*In a more recent work (*Sprachkunst der Lamang* [Afrikanische Forschungen 8], Glückstadt: Augustin, 1980), he covers this and other genres of *Ein-Satz-Literatur*, e.g. riddles, in much more detail.

C. H. Kraft, ***Chadic Wordlists***, 3 Vols. Marburger Studien zur Afrika- und Asienkunde, Serie A: Afrika, Bände 23-25, Berlin: Dietrich Reimer 1981, DM84. Volume I ("Plateau-Sahel"), pp. iv, 261; Volume II ("Biu-Mandara"), pp. ii, 196; Volume III ("Biu-Mandara" et al.), pp. ii, 251.

During 1966-67, Charles Kraft spent a year in northeastern Nigeria collecting lexical data on Chadic languages, with the help of several research assistants. The result was a set of word lists, each 434 items in length, from 63 languages, 59 of which are Chadic (the other four are Niger-Congo). The same 434 item list for Hausa and for Bade, also Chadic languages, are included in Volume I. The Hausa list was the basis of elicitation for most of the other languages; the Bade list was supplied by the author of this note.

Though these lists are a valuable resource, they do need to be used with caution. By Kraft's own admission, this is "raw data", collected by people who did not know the languages. Where independent evidence is available, one can see that transcriptions are phonetically a little rough, but the fact that all the field workers had linguistic training makes the trustworthiness of the lists far superior to that of lists collected by explorers, colonial officers, etc., especially in recognizing crucial distinctions such as those between glottalized vs. non-glottalized stops and palatal vs. lateral fricatives. Each list is accompanied by a "phonemic analysis" and notes on phonology, but in most cases these are simply an articulatorily arranged inventory of symbols used with tentative remarks on distribution.

Perhaps more problematic than phonetic inaccuracies is lack of any morphological analysis. While some morpheme breaks become obvious on inspection, especially in the verbal system, where the same prefix or suffix is repeated time and again, knowledge of the language is necessary in other cases to know what an informant has actually said. For example, in Gude, under 'fever', the list gives màb$_\omega$r̃na. This actually means 'headache' and is analyzable as màbúr ('one which chops') < bur- 'chop') + ná 'head'.

The lists themselves are items numbered 1-434; one must refer to the English key in Volume I to know what each item means. The English key is arranged thematically (kin terms together in one section, body parts together in one section, etc.), which is the best arrangement for elicitation. However, the only way to find how some language expresses a certain meaning, e.g. how Higi expresses 'fire', is to scan the English list until that meaning and its number in the list is found. An index in English alphabetical order would have been useful.

Regardless of these shortcomings, Chadicists and others interested in Chadic data for comparative purposes should welcome the publication of these lists after they have lain so many years in limbo, through no fault of their compiler. Most of these languages still remain unstudied despite the burgeoning Chadic field. Even in language areas where fairly thorough research has been done, there are lists from closely related dialects which give comparative insights, e.g. the Bole list is from the Gombe dialect whereas the Bole material in Lukas' work (esp. "Die Personalia und das primäre Verb im Bolanci [Nordnigerien]," *Afrika und Ubersee* 54:237-286, 1970/71; 55:114-139, 1971/72) is from the Fika dialect. [R.G.S.]

Jean Margain, ***Essais de sémantique sur l'hébreu ancien.*** Monèmes fonctionnels et autonomes, Modalités (Comptes Rendus du Groupe Linguistique d'Etudes Chamito-Sémitiques, Supplément 4). Paris: Geuthner, 1976, 196 pp., map.

This is a thorough study of the use of many grammatical words in Classical Hebrew. Beside synchronic statements, the diachrony is given a great deal of attention. Each chapter is chronologically divided into a section on pre-exilic and exilic usage, one on post-exilic and one on mishnaic phenomena. The titles of the chapters, in English translation, are: I. *ʔeṣɛl* and the expression of proximity, II. *ʔašɛr* and *šɛ-*, III. *ʔab̶ål* and the expression of the adversative, IV. The morpheme *-åʰ* and the expression of "motion toward", V. *lårob̶* and the expression of uncountable quantities, VI. *kan* and the expression of place, VII. *kəb̶år* and the expression of 'already', VIII. *šub̶* and the expression of iteration, IX. *yåk̶ol* and the expression of 'to be able'. General conclusions close this well-documented monograph which will have to be consulted by all Hebraists in the future. [R.H.]

Fritz Werner, ***Modernhebräischer mindest Wortschatz*** (Sprachen der Welt), Munich: Max Hueber, 1979, 240 pp.

This little book contains about 1500 entries listed according to the Hebrew alphabet.* Each headword is followed by spelling variants if needed, by a transcription and grammatical information (feminine and plural forms for adjectives, construct state and plural for nouns, conjugated forms for verbs, etc.). Further given are antonyms if relevant, references to other related entries and finally little phrases, sentences that illustrate the typical uses of the headword. All this is accompanied by translations into German. An appendix gives the numerals, measure and weight units, names of geographic units and their inhabitants, and a list of frequent abbreviations. This is a very carefully constructed book, exhibiting scholarly rigor and competence and providing a realistic representation of spoken Hebrew phraseology. The author should be congratulated for all this.

A German-Hebrew word list would have been useful to make this booklet more efficient. Some criticism may be raised also against the transcription. Vocalic length is consistently marked and this is definitely misleading. Dr. Werner is perfectly aware of the fact that such length is relevant only in a very few cases, e.g. *ba:t* 'you (f.sg.) came' vs. *bat* 'daughter', yet he marked it everywhere he felt it phonetically adequate. In the case of [a˙v] 'father', the voiced consonant does indeed provoke some lengthening of the *a*, cf. [af] 'nose', but this is automatic and barely perceptible. The difference of vowels in [gi˙l] 'age' and [ɪm] 'if' is due to the fact that the latter, as a grammatical particle, is most often stressless in context. In isolation or under emphasis, the vowel of 'if' is the same as that of 'age'. This is thus also secondary and better left unmarked. The most important point is the following. Werner consistently transcribes the stressed masculine plural ending as *-ɪm*, creating a potential for a minimal pair. However, none of my Hebrew informants made a phonetic distinction between *taʔim* 'tasty' (transcribed by Werner as [ta'ʔi˙m]) and *taʔim*, the plural of *ta* 'compartment'

*It is to be noted that the pagination and the placement of the title page follow the Hebrew order. In my opinion this was a much happier solution than the more frequent practice where Hebrew has to yield to the standards of the Latin alphabet. The student has to learn on what side a Hebrew book is to be opened.

which in Werner's system should be [ta'ʔɪm]. This is not to say that there is no problem here—the distribution of the timbres [i] and [ɪ] will require some further research.

A few more objections along these lines could be raised, but this would come close to caviling, considering the merits of the general arrangement and presentation.

I understand that an English version of this book is foreseen. I am sure that its appearance will be welcomed by teachers and learners of Modern Hebrew. [R.H.]